The Manly Art of Seduction

How to Meet, Talk to, and Become Intimate with Anyone

Perry Brass

Belhue Press

Belhue Press, First Edition

Copyright 2010 © Perry Brass

Published in the United States of America by:

Belhue Press
2501 Palisade Avenue, Suite A1
Bronx, NY 10463

Electronic mail address: belhuepress@earthlink.net

Cover and inside book design by Tom Saettel
Cover photo by Stanley Stellar.
Cover photo model: David Handsome

ISBN: 978-1-892149-06-0

ISBN: 1-892149-06-0

Library of Congress Control Number: 2009907411

BISAC category code: SEL034000 (SELF-HELP / Sexual Instruction)

SEL016000 (SELF-HELP / Personal Growth / Happiness)

Publisher's Cataloging-in-Publication
(Provided by Quality Books, Inc.)

Brass, Perry.
    The manly art of seduction : how to meet, talk to,
and become intimate with anyone / Perry Brass. -- 1st
ed.
        p. cm.
    Includes bibliographical references.
    LCCN 2009907411
    ISBN-13: 978-1-892149-06-0
    ISBN-10: 1-89214-906-0

    1. Sex instruction for gay men. 2. Gay men--Sexual
behavior. 3. Flirting. 4. Intimacy (Psychology)
5. Seduction.   I. Title.

HQ76.1.B73 2009   306.77'086'642
                            QBI09-600156

"The human heart is vast enough to contain all the world."

Joseph Conrad, *Lord Jim*

For those seekers of the heart, and for all the men and women who have shared their love with me and have brought me to this place. But especially for Jeffrey Lann Campbell and Marc Collins, who are with me everyday. And, most gratefully, for Dave Singleton, Ken Page, Jerry Kajpust, Tom Saettel, Robert W. Cabell, Robert Woodworth, and Hugh.

Other Books by Perry Brass:

Sex-charge (poetry)

Mirage, a science fiction novel

Works and Other 'Smoky George' Stories

Circles, the sequel to Mirage

Out There: Stories of Private Desires. Horror.
And the Afterlife

Albert or The Book of Man,
the third book in the Mirage series

Works and Other 'Smoky George' Stories,
Expanded Edition

The Harvest, a "science/politico" novel

The Lover of My Soul, A Search for Ecstasy
and Wisdom (poetry and other collected writings)

How to Survive Your <u>Own</u> Gay Life,
An Adult Guide to Love, Sex, and Relationships

Angel Lust, An Erotic Novel of Time Travel

Warlock, A Novel of Possession

The Substance of God, A Spiritual Thriller

Carnal Sacraments, A Historical Novel of the Future

TABLE OF CONTENTS

Foreword

Why did I write this book, and who is it for?

Before I answer those questions, let me tell you: Men are *not* supposed to be seductive.

That's a lesson I learned early on in life, and contradicting that lesson is something I have used to my own benefit through a great deal of it. I have used it mostly because I have gone against the grain of what men are supposed to be (unthinking and unfeeling, insensitive especially to their own feelings, and to those of others) and I've loved it. I have enjoyed being seductive and have learned what I can do with it, and what I cannot do with it: in other words, the uses and limits of this type of behavior. But, most beautifully, seduction has given me an understanding of being in control in situations that leave many men feeling robbed of power, weak, and silent.

I was, I admit, a seductive child (and I believe there are many of us), and then a seductive teenager, and a seductive young adult. Later, I learned that being a seductive *older* adult could be wonderful, too. What it basically says is that you haven't given in to the prejudice that you now have to lock away your feelings, sexual and otherwise, behind a fortress of your own "mature" years. Too many older adults do that; they feel they are now too "old" to be seductive.

Or, to be gladly, happily, seduced.

I wrote this book after writing *How to Survive Your Own Gay Life*, believing that we are now in a terrible state of disconnectedness; that is, people don't connect anymore. As the great (and gay) writer E. M. Forster put it at the beginning of *Howards End*, one of the outstanding novels of intimacy in English: "Only connect." *Howards End* was published in 1910, when England was choking in rigid rules of class difference, decorum, and silence about sex. Today, we are choking in other things: huge anxieties about our survival and safety, the planet's future, and our own well-being, too. Also, in the midst of the cubicle hell of most people's working lives, in their problems with "human literacy" (that is, being able to "read" and understand one another on a personal basis) and their desire to "stay cool" and uncommitted in a constant sales culture, it has become harder for people to connect individually, as well as in groups, in an authentic, satisfying way that does not exclude sexuality but sees sex as part of the whole banquet of human happiness.

So, we have a lot of starvation going on here.

This book is aimed primarily at gay men because I belong to that tribe, but it can be used by anyone, by women of all sexual tastes, and by non-gay men who are adventurous and smart enough to adapt what's in it to their own needs. Seduction, after all, and its promises and thrills are universal. We are being seduced all the time, but usually for the wrong reasons: mostly, to rob us of our deepest, most intimate instincts (and joys), which come from a basic connection with another human being as well as with the inner material of ourselves—but that may be another story which I'll get into later.

All that "seduction" you see on TV, in advertising, and the popular media, the come-ons on every magazine stand ("700 New Ways to Have the Orgasm of Your Life!") are not what this book is about.

You'll notice that there are things for you to do after almost every chapter in this book, so it's a workbook as well as a guide. Please feel free to write in it, or use other sheets of paper to do the exercises, but keep them as part of a journal charting your own progress in mastering the manly art of seduction.

There are some chapters in this book which may offend some people, in that, in a realistic way, I realize that some relationships may be outside the expectations and norm for some of you (most notably the chapters on threesomes, seduction and straight men, and seduction and married men). Please understand that I am not advocating these relationships over other relationships, but feel that realistically, and for your own safety, if you do choose to pursue these situations, some advice about these areas of seductions would be helpful.

My hope is that you can use this book as a guide to fulfilling a natural need in human beings: To connect. To find genuine adventure, excitement, and love, whether in the sack or out of it. And also to expand yourself and come out of the shell of yourself, with valor, truth, and joy!

Perry Brass

1 Seduction Is an Invitation to Intimacy

"I've got you under my skin,
I've got you deep in the heart of me—"

Cole Porter

Sophia Loren was once asked what was the most memorable meeting of her life. "Meeting Cary Grant. We met on a plane. What I remembered first about him was his cologne, a dry, lemony scent and how beautifully close-shaven he was, and also how polite he was. Too many men use rudeness as a strategy for seduction."

Ms. Loren was totally right. Smelling very nice and looking nice are important, but the most powerful asset a man can have for seduction is . . . well, being seductive. And being polite, cordial, warm, and inviting are very much components of that asset. Too often, though, men have no idea how to be seductive or even what seduction is. So here I'll tell you.

Seduction is an invitation to intimacy. It is saying, "I want us to go down that path that will lead to something very nice—at least I'm hoping it will—and I want to show you where the path is, break all the ice standing in the way, and get you to want to go there just as much as I do."

Although intimacy is often seen as pretty informal, usually involving as few clothes as possible (or none at all), seduction as an art form (and it truly is one) is a fairly formal undertaking. In other words, just as an artist has to lay out the colors on his palette before he can begin painting, a good seducer knows that only by arranging the right setting and being in the right frame of mind, can the seduction take place without stalemating into a cold, awkward, and unnerving situation.

Some people might argue that thinking of seduction as an art form, that is "artfully" with some real calculating going on, destroys the spontaneity within meeting someone. The idea that you had it "all thought out in advance" seems like an insult, and some men are so frightened of being considered calculating that they cannot even approach the idea of seducing someone else without exposed nerves and a lot of trepidation.

These men either end up alone a lot, or at the mercy of another person always making the decision to initiate what they both want to happen. If this has been your own hang-up, then you already know how frustrating this is. Mom or Dad might have told you that seductive behavior is evil itself right out of the Devil's own workshop, and they never wanted their little Cub Scout to end up in that role. But they also probably never imagined you'd be hitting the sack with another warm body unless that person was someone you met at a church function and came like Barbie or Ken, that is, without recognizable genitals.

Therefore, let's talk about the first aspect of seduction: knowing when and how to declare your availability.

> "Some enchanted evening, / You may see a stranger /
> You may see a stranger / Across a crowded room—"
> Oscar Hammerstein II

Yes, you may see him, and hear him calling, as the song goes, but how do you let him know that you're really interested in him?

At a party or a bar, this can be achieved by your own *placement* or positioning in that crowded room. So, I'll begin with a few very pointed pointers:

If you are trying to meet someone, don't stick to the center of a crowd of people. Find a comfortable place on the side, and then sit down. If possible, arrange to have an empty seat next to you. If you see someone you feel you're interested in, then see if you can catch his eye. Smile. Smiling is one of the most important aspects of seduction—and also of plain friendliness. A lot of men are so nervous in social situations that they even forget how to smile. A smile is like something they've left at home and can't get to. I'm amazed how many young men no longer smile, like they have some kind of downward facial paralysis. Part of that is the "edgy" sullen culture a lot of guys have bought into, which makes them feel that smiling puts them out of control.

Control of what?

I'll get more into control later, but for now, simply being able to smile shows that you *are* in control. That you're able to enjoy yourself in an atmosphere that others may find taxing and unnerving. So, when you make eye contact, smile. GREAT SECRET TECHNIQUE REVEALED IMMEDIATELY: I know this sounds like a complete cliché, but one very simple way to get yourself to smile is to imagine all the people in the room stark *naked*.

That's right: without a stitch of clothes on.

Now, try to imagine them balancing drinks on their laps, walking around, shoving attitude at each other, while all the time being totally, completely *starkers*. If that doesn't make you smile, try imagining all the judges of the Supreme Court in the same room, the President and Vice President of the US, Prince Charles, the Pope, your fourth grade teacher—anyway, all the people you can't even imagine naked—they're all stark naked too. And, if this doesn't make you smile, then simply imagine yourself naked—and thoroughly enjoying being with this man in the same condition.

Important Note About Smiling

Your smile should *never* be a broad, anxious expression that suggests you're laughing at him (and I'll get to more of that later, too). It should only express your own warmth and happiness at seeing him.

There's an empty chair next to you.

This person is standing up. Your eyes have met.

What do you do?

Run your hand over the empty place by your side. And then look at him, smile, and touch the chair softly, as if he were already sitting in it.

He may get the idea that you want him to walk over to you, or, frankly, he may not. It may be too difficult for him even to imagine this. Some men are too withdrawn socially for them to walk over to you. It's simply an act they're not prepared to do. They might be able to get you to buy a house, but this is a different deal here and that fact—loaded with fears of rejection, of "inappropriateness," and other psychological obstacles and baggage—stands in the way.

But you're smiling, and, hopefully, at this point so is he.

Because the truth is, smiling is contagious, just as having a bad attitude is. So what you're showing is that you don't have one. Instead, you are smiling openly at him. Not laughing, not trying to score points at his expense (something that only *schmucks* do, although there are a lot of *schmucks* out there), but trying to make him feel wanted, attractive, and comfortable.

You, as a seductive person, are trying to do this, but you might want to look at the things that, from his point of view, are standing in the space between the two of you.

One is that he may be there with other friends, so he's feeling that

3

he's deserting them by going over to you. Friends may be a romantically inhibiting factor (he wants to be loyal to them, and conform to their expectations and feelings about what's right. Going off to meet you, even momentarily, may not be one of them).

Conversely, friends may give him a feeling of social security (which we all want), and be a soft, warm "blankey" in a strange place—enough security that he can venture toward you, knowing that no matter what, he's not alone here.

Friends can operate in either role; however, don't count on them encouraging him to meet you. What you want to show is that you're not there to take him away from them. This is simply a warm, nice, friendly encounter, and not an example of hard-core, hell-bent-for-leather, stare-the-man-down cruising.

Close-to-Universal Point Coming Up:

Remember this. You need to lower all stakes, in order to get what you want. Raise them up even an inch, and all bets can soon be off.

However, even if he is alone, he may feel awkward leaving *any* territory he's marked out for himself. This is a sign of his own nerves, and he's showing it. His territory is delineated by the simple fact that you (as well as any other potentially threatening strangers) are not there. So he's not budging. Why?

Very Important Fact About the Male of the Species:

In crowded or tense social situations, men become *territorial*.

Often they feel this is one of their few defenses. It is a return to a primal, even primate behavior. (Spend 10 minutes in any chimp house in a zoo, and you will see it in action.) So he may not want to leave his own territory, even though there is nothing that actually formalizes it as his. There's no sign that says "This Part of Joe's Bar Belongs to Mark." But he doesn't want to believe that.

So Mark, in Joe's Bar, may feel that this particular section of the bar, five feet away from the john, is his, and that, irrational as it is, by leaving it he is also leaving one of the few scraps of security he has. And in situations where you feel easily rejected, where rejection is a common reaction, having a space you feel is your own does add an element of security to your being there. Simple as that.

What can you do to overcome this?

4

Again, very simply, it is now time for you, as the "secure seducer" to walk over to him. You can do this with the feeling that you're *not* giving up *anything* because, in truth, you don't need the territory. You *can* leave your chair, your corner, whatever space you're in and go over to him. Not aggressively, but casually, as if you already do have some slight casual interest in him, even if it's just normal curiosity and a desire to meet him. (And I'll go into exactly how *normal* all this is very soon).

So, walking over to greet him is a purely natural thing to do, and *you* are doing it. You are feeling that doing this is part of your own "kit" of behavior, part of your own personality that you're expressing. You are not being pushy, aggressive, or obnoxious. You are simply being your own naturally curious, interested, and *secure* self.

For some men this idea of standing up and walking over to a stranger takes immeasurable courage. It means that without some prearranged excuse or prior groundwork (what we now call "networking") they are putting themselves on the line to be rejected. But what it really means is that you have the courtesy and control (which I'll talk about later in a chapter on Valor) to do something that you really want to do, which is to meet him.

Still, we have a lot of problems with this. There is something about going out of your way to meet strangers that doesn't seem right to you. Or perhaps even possible.

In fact, it seems downright strange. Or, as they say now, "weird."

In the next two chapters I'll show you that it's not, and what easily allows you to do it, and how you can work on making it simpler and easier for yourself, and also very satisfying as part of your own new, secure, and seductive personality.

CHAPTER 2 · An Important Definition: Intimacy, What Makes It, and What Kills It?

You'll find that I use the term "intimacy" a lot in this book, for the simple reason that for a lot of men intimacy is an extremely hard thing to accomplish. Men who can climb Everest without breaking a sweat find that they cannot get a second date. Men who were making more money in a year than their parents did in a decade feel socially, sexually, and psychologically rejected every day.

Why is this so?

Because intimacy is so difficult for them to achieve.

I'm not crazy about starting off with dictionary definitions, and Webster's standard definition of "intimacy" is a good example of how words lend themselves to a social or political agenda.

Webster: "Intimacy, the condition of being intimate."

What the hell is that? OK, we'll try Webster again: "Intimate: marked by close acquaintance, association, or familiarity."

Again, no real use. Yet, we still need intimacy, and the word itself says what we need. So here's a better definition for you:

Intimacy: a closeness with yourself and others energized
by your deepest social, sexual, or psychological feelings.

In other words, it's allowing someone into that interior landscape that most of the time you keep guarded. It's a landscape of feelings, wishes, dreams, and secrets, that special place of our constant inner childhood and the blossoming of our adulthood, and it is a place that in our most beautiful "heart of hearts" we *do* want to share. Because sharing this place makes us happy, although it also brings with it the risk of rejection, of not being understood, of not being loved for who we are, of not being seen as the self we both protect and treasure: that real, deepest self.

This is a tall order, and so we often do anything possible to lead others away from both that genuine inner self, and from any deeper intimacy or closeness with it. Artists and poets, writers and composers, have used that inner self as the source of their material for centuries; and often they are no better at sharing a genuine intimacy than anyone else is.

But once you have opened yourself up to this sharing (on no matter what level; or what kind of experience opens it up for you—a social one, a sexual one, a religious or intimately spiritual one), you are also opening yourself up to a great and delicious happiness.

It is something you can literally taste, experience, or feel inside.

And it feels very good.

You would think then that people would be opening themselves up to intimacy all the time, and the truth is that many men spend a lot of time and effort making what appears to be a real attempt to do so. They are out there cruising their sweet asses off, rushing to clubs, or singles weekends, or instant dating groups and seminars, trying to open the door to this payoff of intimacy that they want so much. And instead they find that too often the door is slamming very hard behind them.

So here we have the problem of intimacy killers, and what they (or even you) may be doing to produce them.

Some common intimacy killers (I call these the "bad U" problems, as in):
Cru*d*eness.
R*u*deness.
And bad-attit*u*deness.

Crudeness and rudeness have now become common parts of our social landscape. Basically, what they say is, "I have to come first, to prove that I'm here." Because you are so insecure, you always have something to prove: like how important you are, how smart you are, how with-it you are, and how bullying you can be to get your own way. A guy who on a date stays on his cell phone is basically telling another man, "I have to show you how important I am, and how unimportant you are, in order to impress you."

And these same men are *still* complaining about not getting a second date.

There are also the kind of men who have to show you that your feelings are unimportant, and to do so he has to hammer every attitude and opinion he's ever had into you, until you simply stop listening. These kind of men are walking intimacy killers. Nothing you do interests them, so in the middle of a night-long monologue about themselves, why should he ask anything about you?

Or, the kind of man who is always right, and needs to be right so much that he cannot even imagine ever being wrong. I have often thought there is a certain pleasure in being wrong and being proved that way by someone you are interested in: let *him* have that moment of seeing that he is now influencing *you*, giving you something to think about, something new to know. In our hypercompetitive world where being right on the job is a constant, being wrong in an intimate situation can have a certain joy to it. You are being opened up to something new. A new feeling or idea. Even a new experience, one you thought you'd never allow yourself to have. If you are one of those men who can never be wrong, you may find yourself more alone now than ever: a re-occurring problem with many successful men.

However, just as rudeness *and* crudeness can be intimacy killers, the opposite can also work to murder it: men who are constant models of "virtue," social correctness, and relentless political correctness. (They know more about the oppression of every living creature than any living creature has ever known; and they will impress your own "cruelty" and "insensitivity" on you until you can't wait to get the hell away from them.)

In other words, any display of genuine reactions or feelings on your part will be quickly squashed by Goody Two-shoes. These men are in a constant "consciousness raising" situation and you soon find that you can never come up to their level of Universal Awareness. There is something about the gritty, sweaty, sometimes even delicious hardness of life that appalls them, and safe up there in their little ivory towers, they hate it.

These same men have a cousin who is just as inept at achieving intimacy as they are: Good Sport Joe. You have probably met a couple of Joes, been introduced to them, and maybe even someone has tried to pair you up with one.

Joe's a brick. He's an almost cartoon version of the "regular guy," who comes off like a manikin right out of some preppy clothing catalogue

(J. Press comes to mind), and in his ever-present good-sportiness can't understand anyone whose feelings are not as unavailable as his are. He may be adorable, in great shape, and a lifelong Scout, but getting past that facade of constant sporty adolescent conformity (and *love*, I hate to tell you, can sometimes be very *un*sporting) is a job few willingly undertake for very long.

All of these men are in a bad state, and some of them really need to get help not simply on their famous "intimacy" issues, but on the impossibility of their ever approaching or inviting intimacy.

Real intimacy. Real sharing of that sometimes difficult, inner space that produces genuine love and trust.

WORK FOR YOU: Keep in mind your own intimacy-killing attitudes and moves. Start to write them down. Begin with your own need to be right at all times (I know, you never have that!), or what you will do to keep other people (and yourself) from feeling what they (and you) truly need or want to feel.

WORK SPACE:

_____

_____

_____

_____

_____

_____

_____

_____

_____

_____

3 Meeting People Is *Natural.*

"A scout has to be able to notice small details just as much by night as by day and he has to do this chiefly by listening, occasionally by feeling or smelling."
Lord Robert Baden-Powell, *Scouting for Boys,* 1908

Meeting new people in an opening and welcoming way is an innate aspect of intimacy, but our society is now "stranger-phobic." Being a stranger is no longer exciting, desirable, or interesting. It's like we all grow up hating and fearing the "new boy in class." The old idea of the handsome stranger walking into town and everyone being naturally curious about him is over.

This shoots in the head the plots to many classic Westerns.

Strangers are no longer considered fresh air from the outside, or exciting adventurers along the highways of life. Instead they are considered potential threats, even though, in truth, this has *always* been true. Any human being can be a threat to you, including someone you've known most of your life. The vast majority of murders in the U.S. are committed by people who know their victims, not by strangers. But, the idea that the "right" stranger can be an invitation to excitement or satisfaction, well, at the present that's a pretty weird idea.

However, even though our society is now more stranger-phobic than it's ever been (for years, Americans were considered to be hospitable, open, and welcoming; Europeans the opposite), the truth is that human beings really do like, and even crave, meeting other humans. It's the reason why all societies, from the most primitive to the most sophisticated, have rituals and ways of meeting, and the people within these societies find meeting new people interesting, satisfying, and exciting.

They travel to meet new people, go on cruises to do it, join clubs to do it, do it through business, religious, and political life. They walk dogs to do it, play cards to do it, buy new clothes to do it, get their own pages on MySpace, Face Book, and umpteen other "social networking" sites (a new term for an older one: *cruising*) to do it—anyway, you get the idea. Birds of a feather do flock together, and a large number of these birds are on an ambitious, eagle-eyed lookout for new birds all the time.

Humans have this hunger to meet, but we carry a great number of inhibitions and anxieties about it as well. So there is a basic contradiction at work: We *want* to meet new people, but we put up barriers to doing it. Sometimes the barriers are real, as in joining exclusive country clubs to keep unwanted strangers out. And sometimes the barriers are just psychological, that sense that "This just *isn't* done."

But since meeting new people is still a basic human drive, we have also devised numerous ways to lower those barriers that keep you from meeting in order to allow you to have a "normal" amount of trust doing it. Therefore, even the expensive country club does allow the "right" people in, and even the most defensive people can at some point find some way out of the fortified towers they've built for themselves.

One direct way of lowering these barriers is finding areas of commonality. Like I said, you all love dogs, you're walking them. And you love *Star Wars*, collect baseball cards, come from Indiana, and were once Boy Scouts. Or—

You belong to the same fraternity, friends-of-Dorothy fan club, are all gay and love dogs and *Star Wars*, collect Lacoste shirts; and you *all* have hotel reservations for Mr. International Leather Weekend in Chicago.

As you can see, one main reason people form organizations of any sort is to drop the "stranger bar" as low as possible, and to be able to establish a reasonable amount of trust. Since people want to meet each other so much, organizations that establish common interests and experiences tear down some of the barbed wire that keeps distrust working. This does not mean that everyone then is automatically trustable, but it does mean that you can allow yourself to relax a bit in the presence of people who, nonetheless, are still strangers to you.

Also it means that other people can now fit more securely into what I call your own "Self Myth." This is the road map you can start using to be seductive.

WORK FOR YOU: Think of six interests you have that you can use to bring people closer to you. Do not include your work among them, unless your work is also your pleasure. If it is, then include it. But include things that you may overlook, such as cooking, music, pets, travel, reading, movies, collecting, shopping, saving money (yes, sometimes saving money can become a wonderful bond), walking, dancing, politics— just to name a handful.

Now, think of six interests you don't have, or you never thought you might have, and how allowing yourself to have them could open you up to new experiences. Examples: baseball, if you've never been interested in it; opera (there's a reason why so many guys are crazy about it); wrestling; running; birdwatching; medicine; health; gambling; skin diving; speaking another language. Try to replace the idea that you could never even *think* about these things.

WORK SPACE:
Your interests—

_____

_____

_____

_____

_____

_____

New interests you don't have yet—

_____

_____

_____

_____

_____

_____

4 The Self Myth, What It Is and How Important It Is

Your "Self Myth" is basically the story you tell about yourself, and the clear but often unconscious image of you in that story. Another term used for this is your "self map," but I think that is too physical, too based on how you look and how others perceive you. Your Self Myth is a deeper thing, and it affects the very core of you and how you operate in the world. In your Self Myth, self-perception is important, but more important is that you are constructing the myth yourself, although others certainly can help.

First, though, you need to understand what a myth is. A myth is not a story that is untrue. A myth is a story that is used to explain basic truths, often truths that cannot be explained literally. For instance, why do we need love so much? How did we arrive in our places in the world? What is God? How can God be understood?

These questions (and many more) are answered by myths.

What myths do is explain a truth that is already there, or perceived to be there. We do need love; no matter how you slice it, it is an important need. And we did arrive in our places in the world, but exactly how will always be a mystery. We do want to understand God (or some concept close to it) and somehow, we do feel that God can be understood. These are all truly complicated issues and situations, but myths set up a framework for their explanations, and therefore they are important products of human consciousness.

What the Self Myth sets up is a scenario in which you are the main player, actor, and protagonist. The Self Myth allows you to see yourself as your self. That is, a "self" that you can actually identify, one that is (ideally) different from your parents, your family, your friends and coworkers. In truth, too many of us do not really separate ourselves enough from the latter group, but in the Self Myth, you will find that you are the hero of your *own* story: as in fact, you *are*.

A good Self Myth allows you to feel confident and secure enough to do what as an adult you want to do, and feel that you need to do. You do not establish the Self Myth overnight; it is something you allow yourself to have, sometimes with the encouragement of others (and I include myself here), but mostly with your own encouragement. What fuels the Self Myth is your own imagination, your own healthy sensitivity to yourself (and others), and your own ability to express your need to be happy. This, in itself, is a healthy need that is often neurotically cut off to us either by our own problems, or by others.

(I will write more about the Self Myth in the next chapter on valor, but I will refer to the Self Myth and valor often in this book.)

What you want to do is recognize your own need for happiness, and work on things that allow happiness to happen, instead of neurotically rejecting it on the basis that you "don't deserve" happiness, your parents never had it, therefore you shouldn't. Or, you're engaged in "sin," so happiness is definitely *out* for you. Or, the world is *so* bad, how can anyone be happy—just to name a few of the bad Self Myths (or baggage) that people collect around themselves and *schlep* with them.

Remember: If myths are the innate stories of human beings, your own Self Myth is the innate story of a very unique person: you.

The Self Myth includes the story that you left home and made a life for yourself despite all the odds and obstacles against it. It includes the value you give yourself, and the value you want to have—something no one should take away from you, no matter what his or her motives (or excuses) are.

It should include your own tender feelings toward yourself and toward others, and the challenges you feel you face, or that you give yourself. It should also include others who've helped you along your path, those "angels" who appeared at the right time, sometimes through sheer fortune and accident; or who were there all along, either through the "will of God," or just good fortune. It also includes the fact that you could recognize their importance in your life, and see how they fit into the pattern of your life, your own place in the world, and how they have affected your thoughts and actions.

The Self Myth is what allows you to face new challenges, to take on new opportunities, and to openly find and bring toward you the satisfaction you want. So the Self Myth is part of your own birthright, and very much a part of seduction.

It is what fortifies you enough to be seductive. This is not to say that the Self Myth alone can do it. There are limits to any myth, yours or others. But recognizing that you are part of a very human pattern, and that what you want is natural to all human beings is utterly strengthening. *It means that being alone and unhappy is not an ordained destiny for you.* Your Self Myth will tell you so. And, with some of the techniques in this book you will be able to be the seductive, sexually and emotionally enriched man you want to be.

A very *important* part of the Self Myth is opening this story up to allow another person into it. In fact, as your imagination makes the Self Myth more wonderful (and larger), you will start to see a larger number of people as being desirable and open to seduction. If you've been blocked by having a "type" that was as narrow as a toothpick, this attitude will change.

Something to remember: men with extremely narrow ranges of "type," are often men who are not sexually successful. They have boxed themselves into a corner, often out of rejection. They can always assert: "He wasn't my type."

And they were right. He probably wasn't, especially if "Mr. Narrow Range" began the seduction process by putting the other man down. Many men who play "hard to get" are often terrified of being "gotten"— that is, of being seen for what they are: totally insecure inside. They are that, no matter how they look or act.

The Self Myth works against this. It says, "I know who I am. I can tell my own story, fairly, warmly, with justice to myself. And I can allow other men into it, including many men I haven't even met yet."

What the Self Myth allows is real intimacy with yourself. You can enjoy this intimacy, instead of being afraid of it. You can see how much you really do like yourself, on a real and justified level.

This intimacy allows you to get close to yourself, as well as someone else. It also allows for your own natural shyness, and your own fears. You don't have to be afraid of either anymore. You can see them as natural parts of yourself, and within your own Self Myth.

Please note: Liking yourself does not mean being narcissistically involved with an image of yourself that is completely unreal. This narcissistic involvement can also include men who constantly put themselves down. They have invented an inferior image of themselves that is also unreal.

So the Self Myth allows you to trust yourself, knowing that you will make mistakes. You may come off as being fumbling and unsure sometimes—who doesn't? But that, again, is a part of the real you that you can understand and see.

Trusting yourself is very important in seduction: trusting your own good intentions, and knowing that meeting men for sexual and emotional happiness is not a bad intention at all. So keep in mind that the art of seduction is a good one in your hands.

Now all you have to do is allow it to work. (I'll discuss how in the next chapter.)

WORK FOR YOU: See your life in five "Acts": (1) Your birth and early years. (2) Your time beginning to see yourself as a separate person. (3) Your education, and the end of "formal" education. (4) Your going forth into the world, and what you learned there. (5) And where you are now. Can you capture your beginning "acts" up to now, that is, the start of your own Self Myth? How positive has it been? How positive can you make it? Write down some ideas about this, and keep them until you finish this book.

WORK SPACE:

_____

_____

_____

_____

_____

_____

_____

_____

_____

_____

_____

_____

_____

5 Fulfilling the Hunger for Valor

It is impossible to talk about seduction without also bringing up *valor*. In fact, when I'm asked what is the most important thing in forming any genuine relationship, either with yourself or someone else, I often quickly answer one word: Valor.

Valor seems so old-fashioned, so completely out of date, that many men can barely speak the word without smirking or becoming embarrassed. The word seems to call for dealing with something that many men now find *so* missing that its stark absence is too painful, too obvious, and too embarrassing.

So they want to joke it away.

Valor appears to date back to old Gary Cooper movies, dinner jackets and stiff collars and even stiffer manners and attitudes: a world outside our enforced habits of bland, casual (and often lonely) familiarities that leave little room for developing deeper attachments and intimacies. Our world, which seems blander, colder, and more isolating, in a word, *hates* valor (although I have a feeling that in today's harder economic climate, valor is ready to make a comeback).

The feeling is that calling forth valor is not *cool*, and will make you stick out. But, valor calls for a meeting with your own ability to *value* yourself. Therefore, it is an important part of forming a good, useful, and very healthy Self Myth.

People say, "Valor is bravery," and often valor is associated with brave acts, but in truth valor provides the environment in which bravery can take place. It provides the strength of character necessary for bravery as well as for securely asserting yourself.

Valor comes from the French word for "value," and "to be strong"— we get our words "validate" and "valorize," meaning "to infuse something with value and courage," from *valor*. In turn, valor comes from an even older French term, dating back to Chaucer's time, meaning to "control" or to "rule." *Valor*, then, is an attitude of connection with and control of yourself that allows bravery (and therefore, a control of circumstances) to happen.

This control may simply be that you *can* act first. Since in most circumstances you can only be in control of yourself, your own initiation of actions will set things into play capable of producing what you want, therefore allowing you the *control* you desire.

This is difficult for many people to deal with, because if you are the first to make a move, it means that you must also accept the consequences of your actions, and for many *gay* men (in particular, though frankly not any more so than most people), this brings up that terrifying demon *rejection*. The demon of rejection may come from many things: the terrifying demons of your rejection as a child, or the fear of rejection simply for being gay, being different, therefore being unacceptable. (That taunt from kids, "You're so *gay!*" comes right up.)

I'm sure you can imagine these demons of rejection yourself right now. And you can give faces to them: all the people who've hurt you with rejection, or have left a shadow, a phantom of rejection, lurking behind them without a face.

This phantom of rejection, I feel, has a genuine presence in the daily lives of many men. I know because I have felt his evil presence myself. But if we have the ugly demons of rejection and their phantoms (who look like something right out of our worst horror movies), I want us also to see valor as being a wonderful knight, the brave Knight of Valor. I want to personify him as such, because this worthy Knight says that you can go forward without fear of rejection because—and this is the most important aspect of valor, and it should become an important part of your own Life Myth—*you will not reject yourself.*

Please remember this. *You will not reject yourself.* I cannot stress it strongly enough.

In other words, you have built enough value into yourself that you will see yourself as valorous, as *capable* of the very bravery you deserve.

For many men, this is terrifying. It makes mixed martial arts look easy—because it means that you must not only start an action, but be so strong that its consequences will not destroy you.

Before reading this book, many of you could only see the social or sexual consequences of your actions as being hurtful or rejecting: they were that anxiety-provoking. *If you start something, you'll end up paying for it.* This little voice inside you warns you of that constantly. You keep hearing that terrible "Mom's voice" inside you, saying, "It serves you right, Buster! You went out on a limb, and I was waiting right there to saw it off for you. Now look where you are!"

We have all heard that voice. I have as well, and the strangest thing is that when I hear that voice now, either from myself or from others, I know exactly where it's coming from.

It is not coming from the speaker, but from those toxic elements inside him. The demons of blame, rejection, and past hurt.

It's time to start ejecting *them.*

The real results of initiating action may be wonderful and energizing, but that phantom fear of its consequences—with the phantom clutching the fatal knife of rejection—keeps many men from exercising their own needs for valor. And we do need it. It is that very need, starving inside us, that keeps many men from being active and seductive.

Men hunger for valor, with a huge, tender, secret spot inside them that yearns for that Knight of Valor to approach them, love them, and in doing so, even become them; for them to merge with him, and then experience his value as theirs. We see this hunger in the constant wish-fulfillment stories that have excited us over thousands of years, those stories of heroes, action, adventure, revenge, and love. Much of what we call "entertainment" is based on these stories: the hero whom we want to claim us, and then become a part of us, to enter into our emotional core. Powerful, tender, vulnerable at moments, protective, he animates so many of our stories and dreams, and personifies the very strength of love we desire, a love from outside as well as from within.

Gay men especially want this, although non-gay men want it as well, but have a harder time identifying the need. Its stark emotional nakedness embarrasses them at a time when men are basically allowed only one real response to each other: constant, "24/7" competition. It is extremely hard for men to lower the bar of this competition and be themselves, and the hunger this has left, for genuine closeness and warmth, is palpable.

You can feel it whenever men get together. But being able to reduce this hunger through genuine contact has become a skill few men develop anymore.

I describe this hunger for valor, this starvation, as the result of men lacking what I call "emotional currency," or in plain language, emotional resources. They lack the inner emotional resources to expend on genuine closeness and intimacy with other men. This lack, this vacuum, often leads to depression, drug and alcohol dependency, sadness, and chronic feelings of aloneness.

19

This has destroyed generations of men—and I believe it has led to the environment of constant war we're in. But, in some ways, it has reinforced and armed a generation of *gay* men because we can allow our own needs for valor to emerge, as we did during the AIDS epidemic when often we had to act in valorous, truly courageous ways.

The problem is, how do you encourage your own valor, if you can barely recognize what valor is and how much it's missing?

Some Questions About Missing Valor

Are you always waiting for someone *else* to make the first move, socially or sexually? A move toward creating deeper friendships, and the more profound relationships you feel you'd like to have but can't attract?

Are you locked in a passive pattern of waiting?

Are you haunted by fear of rejection, so that making the first move has become too scary for you?

Are you incapable of truly recognizing acceptance? When you're with other men, are you convinced that rejection is always around the corner waiting for you?

Does rejection seem more real to you than acceptance?

And, if and when rejection does come, do you feel helpless, incapable of confronting it or dealing with it? Do you reject yourself, as well, when rejection makes itself known? Are you incapable of going into a situation of possible rejection and asking for honesty?

Are you easily manipulated by the coarseness or callousness of others, and feel helpless dealing with their lack of sensitivity?

When things go wrong (as they can in the course of any relationship), do you automatically feel that you must be at fault? Do you beat up on yourself without redeeming your own value, as well as the value of the relationship itself? Is it impossible for you to say the relationship was important, I'm an important part of it, therefore, I will be valorous enough to step back into it?

If you answer "Yes" to these questions, then there is a need for valor in your life, and you are not fulfilling that need. You may not even be recognizing valor in others, or what you can do to bring valor into your own life and relationships.

Working on Valor

First, I want you to understand that valor comes from genuine intimacy with yourself. If you cannot spend time with yourself without constant "entertainment" from outside—and by "entertainment" I mean that commercial circus of canned, fake adventure, fake intimacies, and fake relationships all around us—it will be hard for you to develop a feeling of valor and have it revealed to you. It may take a while to strip away some of the "entertainment," but the fact that you want valor in your life is important. In the next chapter I will deal with developing this extremely important sense of intimacy with your self. But first, I want us to do some work identifying valor. So try to do the exercise on the next page.

WORK FOR YOU: Can you remember a valorous situation from your childhood or youth, when someone "stepped" in and made you feel valuable, worthy, and recognized? Was this someone a relative, a teacher, an older person, a friend?

If you cannot remember this kind of situation, can you identify one where you openly missed this happening? When you yearned for it? How has that yearning affected you now?

WORK SPACE:

_____

_____

_____

_____

_____

_____

_____

_____

_____

6 Genuine Intimacy with Yourself

"I loaf and invite my soul,
... at my ease observing a spear of summer grass."
Walt Whitman, "Song of Myself"

When I talk about intimacy with yourself, the first thing that comes to mind for a lot of men is masturbation. This is sad, not because masturbation is bad, but because "self love" in this instance just does not go far enough. Intimacy with yourself is experiencing the genuine, separate person within you. That is, yourself as a person capable of strength, goodness, and resilience.

Unfortunately, many of us have a hard time seeing ourselves at all.

We see "advertisements" for ourselves, with lots of the fake effects we prop up in front of others, but spending time in any genuine self-intimacy has become a too-expensive luxury we feel we can't afford. It's not cool. It won't get us on *American Idol*. And, frankly, it makes us feel too vulnerable. Some of us try for this self-intimacy through spirituality and religion, which have become two of the few avenues of this kind left in our world. But "getting to know yourself," a process that used to be very much a part of growing up into an individualized adult, has been replaced by addictive TV watching, shopping as a form of "self-expression," trying to outguess and beat the state of economics in order to survive, redoing your MySpace page, as well as trying to figure out what latest fad is going to be the next "you."

In order to find your own *value*, it's important to set aside some very valuable time simply to be yourself.

After all, how valuable are you if you cannot set aside time for *you*? And by this I don't mean time spent in boredom and loneliness, but time that is engaged and interested in the world around you, and inside you. This means a time for activities that generously allow you to expand.

In my book *How to Survive Your Own Gay Life*, I talked about allowing yourself time for yourself, to listen to your own thoughts, and to learn to genuinely love yourself in a way that sees yourself clearly, without all the usual narcissistic roadblocks, such as: "I've worked so hard for me, my muscles, my toys, and my money, who the hell needs anyone else?"

Some other ways to spend time developing self-intimacy: reading great books instead of junk literature. (Leave the Jackies, Suzanne and Collins, to other times). Some books that I feel are incredible guides to intimacy with yourself would include *Howards End* by the wonderful gay writer

E. M. Forster, who also wrote the queer classic *Maurice*; *Women in Love* by D. H. Lawrence; *The Hours* by Michael Cunningham (which, by the way, was made into a movie beautiful enough to stand on its own); and *A Single Man* by Christopher Isherwood. In all of these books, the message is knowing yourself in a world that works hard to keep you from doing it. You can also join a reading group to get some guidance. Reading is one of the most self-intimate of acts. You are involved in a dialogue with the author and your inner self, and that inner self can really come out exploring literature. Poetry, "the Now that's always news," as Ezra Pound put it, is another tool guiding you toward yourself; as are classical music, some forms of jazz, and even pop "standards." Hobbies can put you into contact with this inner self, such a bird-watching and hiking outdoors; and of course the arts, such as painting, dance, and drama. Whether you are participating in them, or just looking at them with all your senses and feelings open, the important thing is that you are now engaged in a dialogue with your own self as it expands and opens to others and other feelings.

Exercise and sports also can connect you in a very deep way with your self, if you don't let fear of failure destroy that connection. Competition can be very sensual and exciting, but at a certain point, it can become wearing and stressful, especially when you are competing not just with others but with your own starved needs for attention and recognition. Too often, this becomes, a problem with athletes. Once all the cheering has stopped, what are they left with?

I want you to be left with a deeper, more satisfying sense of yourself.

Once inside this environment of your "Self"—that is, of you as a separate person *you* can experience—you may discover aspects of you that you feel are lacking (and the fear of this scares a lot of people away from any kind of self-knowledge), but you will also experience what is genuinely worthy of love and forgiveness. You will also see that no matter what age you are, you've been through a lot already and you can find places in you that have depth, and the wisdom and strength both to grow and change, and simply to be and enjoy yourself.

This will give you some genuine *inner* strength—and support—dealing with rejection. Rejection from others will be balanced by that closeness you already have with yourself, allowing you a real sense of inner security

In other words, most people are not going to be as genuinely *intimate* with you as *you* are with yourself. Now, I said "some" genuine *inner* strength, because rejection *is* difficult to deal with. But it should not be so devastating, so destructive, that it destroys the natural feeling of valor you are experiencing, which will allow you to expand again without closing down.

With this sense of inner strength working, you should be able to achieve what I call a "No Mistakes," attitude—that is, if you have exerted yourself, opened yourself up, and extended your feelings to another person, then no matter how far you fall on your face, it's simply *not* a mistake.

You don't have to *suffer*, you don't have to "pay" for your actions with that "it serves you right!" response so many of us learned as kids. You can look at yourself and say, "I was able to do this. I was able to face my own fears, my own shyness or reserve, and approach someone with openness and kindness." Don't berate yourself if your approach doesn't work. It's not attempting the approach that's a mistake.

The mistake would be not attempting it.

Seducing Your Self

Another beautiful aspect of the manly art of seduction is simply seducing your self. Or, "Self," as I would like to call it. By this I mean that as you become more acquainted with your own powers of being, of seeing yourself as capable, beautiful, and forgiving, your own feelings for you as a separate, worthy, and capable being will increase. This does not mean that you can now use this feeling stupidly and without consideration for others; in other words, become a part of the usual banal and unfeeling narcissism we often see around us. But it does mean that as you get out of the isolating ruts you may have found yourself in before you started this book, and as you start to see and use the art form of seduction, you will also be literally seducing your Self, bringing that self closer to you, coaxing it into more self-confidence and happiness. This is your birthright, and I hope you will claim it.

WORK FOR YOU: What is the most embarrassing situation you've ever been in? Try to call it to mind, and realize it in the perspective of time. Would it embarrass you now? Would you think it was funny, or at least funny in retrospect? What did you learn from it, and what positive energy or feelings can you bring out of it?

WORK SPACE:

_____

_____

_____

_____

_____

_____

_____

_____

_____

_____

7 Working Off Excitement

"Another opening / Another show!"
Cole Porter, Kiss Me, Kate

Besides having things in common like hobbies, or interests (opera, baseball, collecting antiques, or seeing all of the *Lord of the Rings* movies), one thing that opens up the field of intimacy (and seduction) is shared excitement, something you can sink your teeth into and that others are sharing with you.

Boys know this about sports, which is why in the culture of adolescents (and those who remain that way forever), sports are of such urgent importance. It's one safe way that men can vent many feelings of passion and intimacy with other men, and keep it "kosher." The hit Broadway play *Take Me Out*, about the difficult but exciting intersection of gay men and baseball, beautifully revealed that.

If you have something that completely turns you on, it can provide an easy approach to meeting other men, gay or not. And if they are gay, it gives you a much more direct route to opening up feelings of sexual interest. Gay camping, mountain climbing, and other outdoor activities are great ways to do this. These activities combine moments of aloneness with nature and times when "normal" valor can be expressed (like when you jumped into that freezing lake because Harold, who was so cute in hiking shorts, did it first), with some moments of exceptional valor (like when, totally exhausted, *you* helped Bill, who had sprained his ankle, carry his pack). They start your heart pumping, get your blood going, and break down barriers between you and strangers.

Religion (and what has become, too often, its even stranger twin, politics) is another way of doing this. Working on a campaign, a church project, or something very real, very tangible, that causes you and other men to see each other as "brothers in a cause" can be helpful, too.

Strangely enough, an outside crisis is something that allows a fairly instant level of trust to occur, when everyone is thrown into working hard to meet it. I mentioned that the AIDS crisis allowed gay men to show their valor. Men who met during the early years of the crisis could not believe how fast they established intimacy with each other, an intimacy that was emotional, psychological, and sometimes quite sexual.

Anyone who's ever been in a war situation understands this. Suddenly you're meeting dozens—hundreds—of people, with few inhibitions about meeting them, as long as they're on your side! Your own Self Myth becomes as big as the war itself, hence the old idea of the "war story," a story you can share over and over again, bringing people to a closer level of intimacy with you.

Some men will tell you that the best times in their lives were during a war, in the Army. They could forget about their hang-ups, inferiority problems, and the cut of their suits. In these situations, if you just did what was expected of you in the midst of turbulence, a huge amount of bonding would take place.

Often, with sex involved.

My own "war" experiences came during the first several years after the Stonewall Riots (or Stonewall Rebellion) in June, 1969, when I became intensely involved with the radical arm of the gay movement through the Gay Liberation Front and other similar political groups. Suddenly, dozens, even hundreds, of people were my gay and lesbian brothers and sisters, all united and energized, passionately working toward literally inventing a movement known as gay liberation, something that could not even be spoken of a few years before then. The power and excitement of that period has been evoked for other causes, such as gay marriage, but what is important to understand is that things that unite and excite you also bring you closer to people in an intimate way.

As the novelist Evelyn Waugh once said about World War II, "People get into wars in order to be able to do the things that they always wanted to do and could never get away with."

With Waugh's wisdom in mind, remember: Meeting people is natural. It has now become a part of your own Self Myth. And you DON'T have to get into a war to do it.

So get up, go over and meet him.

Because that is the natural thing to do.

WORH FOR YOU: What excites you? Have you ever shared this experience with another person? How did that sharing work out? If you haven't tried sharing it, plan on doing it in the future. Think of how you can share it, and what you can do to plan sharing it.

WORH SPACE:
Plans for sharing—

_____

_____

_____

_____

_____

_____

_____

_____

_____

8 Left, Right, or in the Middle. Other Positions

Previously I said that a good place to position yourself to meet someone is outside a group, on the edge of it. That's true: it is good. However, sometimes you may feel a bit out of it, alienated, and alone there, especially when everyone else is bellying up to the bar, the food, or to congratulate the guest of honor. People who do studies of power positioning have found that in most groups, the most powerful people position themselves in a strategic corner, rather than in the middle of a crowd. Crowds of people become unmanageable, and that is the one thing that power does not want: unmanageability. However, in a seduction situation you are not there to whip out your resume and impress a would-be boss, who may be at a "star table" holding court in a corner.

If you start to feel that nothing is happening, then get up, and start to circulate *slowly*, trying not to get so lost in the thick of the crowd that it becomes difficult for another person to approach you, as well as for you to approach him.

One good thing about crowds is an immediate "crisis" reflex that they often bring out; and, as I said before, a crisis can create a shortcut to intimacy. The fact that you are now thrown together with someone unfamiliar gives you an instant subject to talk about:

You, smiling at him: "Gosh, it's crowded in here."
Him: "It is."
You: "Do you like crowds?"
Him: "No."
You, smiling: "Neither do I. Perhaps we should find a table."

Again, use the situation that you're in and feel natural about it. You can feel secure enough to include him in your plan. He may find this amazing, even shocking, but the attitude that this is a normal thing for you to do is wonderfully impressive. It shows that you have a natural sense of courtesy, and you are extending it to him. You are extending your own sense of valor and showing you are in control.

If he gives you any resistance, don't worry. The resistance may simply be a reflex based on his own insecurity, and he may get over it shortly and walk over to you, if only out of curiosity.

Curiosity, like the desire to meet, is normal and human; it's an excellent component of seduction. We very much live in an Age of Suppressed Curiosity, where most people have little interest in exploring what lies past the first couple of pages of any search engine. It's like a return to the Middle Ages, when the Church said the world was flat, only certain ideas would be permitted, and no curiosity would be permitted past that dogma.

Of course some people *were* more curious, and that was how the New World (and a lot of the Old World) was discovered, along with everything else. So allow your natural curiosity to take its course, as well as that of another man.

However, keep this in mind: in many anxious cruising, networking, or hyper-social situations, men find themselves running faster and faster, like laboratory rats, around a perceived center of excitement that only barely exists. If you find yourself plopped down in the middle of this lunacy, just consider that *you* are now the excitement, and want to share this with someone else—for instance, a particular man you have in mind. Being slightly outside a crowd is good, just as mingling with it can work if you know what you're doing and don't give way to a "crowd-crisis" mentality and the anxiety it provokes. What's important is that you are secure enough in your position and feel in control of it enough to extend yourself toward someone else.

You want to feel that no matter where you are, your presence holds within it something that is valuable, attractive, interesting, and friendly. There may be a little voice within you saying, "Who are *you* kidding?" but you really *do* want to feel this way. And, if you don't, as the old sales adage goes, "Just fake it until you make it." Or, realize that it's possible for you to put on a confident persona, and realize it, too.

As Archie Leach, the young handsome Cockney acrobat who later became known by another name said, "First I invented Cary Grant, then I became him."

But he had to believe in Cary Grant first. And one of the best approaches to feeling this confident is to have some idea of what to say when the time comes to say it.

WORK FOR YOU: Write down three times when you wish you had acted, and did not. You can refer to them by specific names (cousin Jenny's wedding; that guy at the bar in San Francisco), or just give them a close-enough date (April, two years ago). Then, when you finish this book, go back to them, and think how you could have changed what happened.

WORK SPACE:

_____

_____

_____

_____

_____

_____

_____

_____

_____

9 Breaking Out of Shyness, or Ice Breakers

"Though she had long guessed Edgar's intentions
she had not till that afternoon been quite sure
that he would ever bring himself to the point of
speaking and till he did, had felt it unnecessary
to make up her mind what she should answer."

W. Somerset Maugham, *Up at the Villa*

Now, you face the question: What do you say after you say "Hi" or "Hello"?

Or—do you say either?

The answer of course is, "Yes."

Say, "Hi." Or, more formally, "Hello." (I am one of those fogies who hates the "What's up?" bullshit, because it takes you out of the situation. "Hi" is short for saying, "How are you?" which asks a question, bringing both you and the other guy into play. "What's up?" feels cold and distancing. But for some guys "What's up?" works. So, well . . . *cool.*)

Now this is where a lot of guys get into problems, or as they say, *deep shit.*

What do you say after "Hello," without coming off sounding like a complete dork? Before we go into the answer to this question, let's consider the reason *why* the problem has become so much worse for a lot of men, especially a lot of *younger* men.

If you *are* a young man (and we all were once), you know what I'm talking about. First, you're shy. Second, you're not *all* that sure of yourself. And third, you're sure that he's judging you by how smart, clever, and fun you are in those couple of words that follow whatever you said first.

Shy, unsure, and judgmental have always been a part of human nature. Any screwball comedy from the 1930s will show you that, as well as most of the movies of Doris Day or Tom Hanks. No one was shyer and more stammering than Jimmy Stewart, no one managed to say the wrong thing more than Katharine Hepburn. "Shy, unsure, and judgmental" have been around a long time.

Guys today have an added handicap. And for some of them, it is truly crippling. Young gay men today get a large portion of their social (and sexual) cues from porn movies and TV.

In porn movies, everyone performs spectacularly, is humongously endowed, and doesn't have a single problem meeting anyone. On TV, everyone knows exactly what to say, hits the mark perfectly, and scores a perfect bull's-eye zinger with every line—*because all the lines have been written for him.*

When you get a top Hollywood comedy writer to pen your lines and then get the earlier part of the week to rehearse them, you too can come off like a character from *Two and a Half Men* or *How I Met Your Mother*, if that's what you want. But, during a fairly spontaneous natural meeting, your scriptwriter might have the day off, so it'll be up to you to impress—and this is where the rubber hits the road.

Because you can feel awfully socially pressured and *alone*, unless you keep these valuable ideas close in mind.

1) Your own natural shyness and nervousness *can* work for you, if you *don't* get so close to Mr. Right Guy that, being directly in his face, he feels threatened. Give both of you a little space. Don't jump right at him. And of course smile.

2) The fact that you have made the first move is always in your favor. Not his. No matter who's keeping score on the side.

3) And, everyone (except complete sickoes; I'll go into those later) loves the compliment of someone paying attention to him, especially when there is enough space around the compliment not to feel physically or psychologically threatened.

This is very, *very* important.

Just approach. Let him know you're there. Say "Hi," and smile.

Then make a general comment about the setting. Nothing too specific. Nothing so devastatingly clever that this stranger has to feel that he's got to come up to it—and certainly not bitchy.

In other words, no matter where you are, no matter what's going on, even if you're knee-deep in zebra dung and the hostess is passing around something that looks like it came from a Puppy Chow can, don't put the situation down.

Just a little opening comment will do.

"It's really crowded here."

"I guess we're the first ones here."

"Cold tonight, isn't it?"

"Hot outside."

"I like the plants."

"I like that song. Any idea who's singing?"

Engage his eyes, but not so much that you're staring into them, or look like you're searching for the next thing to say.

Now, give him this wonderful little present that only you can give him. Introduce yourself.

Ah, yes. Give him your name, as in: "My name's _____."

Unfortunately some men feel that this is an impossibly difficult thing to do. In our edgy, nervy, *Six Feet Under*-greets-*Grand Theft Auto* society, this show of civility called, "My name is Alex" (or Tom, or Dick, or Harry) is so refreshing that it can make anyone smile.

And what you'll do next is even better. Compliment him. Say something nice.

Not something so overwhelming that it intimidates him and makes him wonder what kind of kook you are—"You are the most beautiful man I've ever laid eyes on in my whole life. And you have the kind of eyes I'd die for!"

Try, "That's a really nice shirt. Where did you get it?"

"I noticed your tie over there."

"I like your haircut."

"I like the way you smile."

And, don't forget "You look interesting."

The last one, if delivered sincerely, without a smirk or a giggle, can deliver a real bull's-eye straight from Cupid's quiver. So many guys today feel that only Brad Pitt and Jude Law (preferably rolled into one) could ever look interesting. And now, suddenly, you're saying they are.

The same goes for: "You're looking attractive."

Say this in a fairly matter-of-fact tone, like you might say this to any number of men. It's something you're used to observing—so again, he doesn't feel put upon, pounced on, and you don't come off as desperate. Keep it low-key. Basically, you're saying you're used to good-looking men, and he's one of them.

In Chapter 11, I will go into the importance of what I call unbidden gifts. Introductions and compliments are very much two of these unbidden gifts. So keep in mind that using them is not inventing the wheel, but part of a dance of intimacy that men have been using for ages, and that continuously fits the music of any age.

If for any reason you feel uncomfortable trotting out a compliment so fast, then you can revert to some of the more tried-and-true lines. Lines that don't go out of style, no matter how corny they sound.

"How do you know Ben and Steve?" (The hosts of the party.)

"Do you come to this bar a lot?"

"Have you been here very long?"

"What are you drinking?" (If it's a beer out of a can, don't try that one.)

You will notice that all of these lines are questions. Questions bring him into the conversation. One of the keys to being a *superb* conversationalist, as Oscar Wilde once noted, is being a good listener. In fact, you don't have to say a word to be considered an excellent talker, if you let him talk.

He may talk a lot out of sheer nervousness, and you may be listening to him a lot because now you're more comfortable and secure than he is.

At this point, you've edged somewhat closer to him, listened to what he had to say for a few minutes, and given him enough space to "expand."

That is exactly what happens when we feel comfortable in the presence of others. He may not expand instantly, but he may go into those wonderful preening gestures that show he is feeling secure enough physically to show off.

WORK FOR YOU: Think of three compliments that you'd love for someone to give you. Have you ever been given them? How would you feel if a stranger came up to you and said exactly that to you? Now, imagine the effect of your compliments on someone else.

WORK SPACE:

_____

_____

_____

_____

_____

_____

_____

_____

_____

10 "Body Language" and Reading It

Any good seducer becomes an excellent interpreter of "body language." Here are some examples of "preening" body language, which shows that a man is actually relaxing under your attention, whether his conversation reveals it or not:

A man who touches his hair, especially combing his fingers through it.

A man who touches his face, especially running his thumb under his chin.

A man who touches the back of his neck, even if he's not looking at you.

These are unconscious signs that, physically, he's starting to feel relaxed and that expansion thing that I talked about is going on. Just observe them. At a certain point, his body may start telling his mind what to do.

In other words, *physically*, he feels comfortable with you. This is a great thing.

Unfortunately, a lot of men are scared of letting their bodies talk for them. They don't trust their own bodies. Sometimes you see this in the rigid, protective way they hold themselves. A good example of this rigid, protective posture is found in the "military posture": chin tucked in, neck straight up, back ramrod straight. This is not a natural way for the body to hold itself, although it does give the effect of being at attention. The opposite of this is the man who slumps constantly, showing that he is allowing his body to become fatigued and to show fatigue. Kids think that slumping is natural. It is not. It also announces to others that you will not pay attention to them, and that you are in a "cool" holding pattern, warding off attention from others.

For many men, the body is something to be whipped into shape at the gym, forced into office spaces it doesn't want to be confined in, and kept up way past its bedtime. That's why we yawn. The body is telling you it's tired. What we are seeing in all these cases is that the body is reacting with a "mind of its own," even when the body's "mind" is simply reflecting its owner's.

But in this case of body language, his body may be saying, "I really like the fact that someone nice is paying attention to me, and showing me that I'm looking good!" Therefore, the body goes into its wonderful, unconscious preening motions. Animals have been doing this for millions of years, and humans are simply following suit.

Some people call this "chemistry," and there is a reality to this. For instance, your body actually smells different when you're upset, angry, or scared, than it does when you are calm, satisfied, or happy. Dogs, the great judges of scent, know this well. A dog that feels you don't like it will attack you. A dog can smell your hostility with a lot more veracity than most people can perceive it by relying on psychological judgments alone.

There is also a kind of basic male body odor that attracts people, especially other men. This is something even straight men will admit if they let their guards down enough. Some people attribute this to pheromones, those attraction-enhancing chemicals the body produces; but some of this chemistry is caused by the fact that when you are in a state of genuine attraction, your own nose and scent nerves become more responsive to smells and those scents become more powerfully attractive.

This is like "essence of erection" coming right through your nose. So you can forget the little blue pill, if you let yourself relax into it! Wow.

WORK FOR YOU: Can you remember a man telegraphing his feelings toward you in a physical way? The feelings can be of anger, hostility, sensuality, attraction, or even uncertainty. Can you attach a physical action to each of these feelings? Now, have you ever tried to keep from telegraphing your own feelings? Which actions or reactions have you tried to suppress?

WORK SPACE:

_____

_____

_____

_____

_____

_____

_____

_____

11 More on Valor, Intimacy, and Seduction: The Importance of Unbidden Gifts

At this point, I want to go further into other basic aspects of intimacy and seduction. Some of this may sound more theoretical than practical, but it's important to getting the foundation set. So please forgive me, but it's time to talk more about that basic idea of gifts.

One of my favorite concepts dealing with intimacy is the importance of unbidden gifts.

What are they? Basically, gifts you don't ask for, but that you recognize and accept. In my youth, we used to call them "stuff that was laid on you." As in, "he laid a joint on me," or "he laid on me this pair of jeans." In other words, I never asked for it, and in a moment of sheer love I was given it.

Unbidden gifts are signals people send out, and the real magic of them comes in recognizing their inner hidden message and value. In other words, they are part of the code and dance of intimacy, and especially of male intimacy.

My favorite story of the unbidden gift comes from the Bible, when Abraham sent his most trusted servant back to the patriarch's birth land to look for a wife for his son Isaac. The servant did as he was instructed, but was not sure what sign would reveal to him a suitable match for Isaac. Then he heard God saying that he should look for a woman who will offer him water at the well, not only for himself, but also for his camels; that is, a young woman who will offer him some bit of unexpected kindness.

The servant finds Rebecca, who out of pure goodness of heart offers to draw water for him and for his camels—an unbidden gift that the servant knows to recognize and value. He sees Rebecca's offer as a signal that she is suitable for his boss's son, and at once offers trinkets of gold to her to show that he, too, is on the up-and-up. I find this a wonderful foil to the pop-culture drivel of shows like *The Bachelor* and *The Bachelorette* on network TV, where potential trophy brides or grooms are sent through a humiliating series of contests, obstacles, and free-flying insults to reveal their rightness, instead of having them show, simply enough, genuine aspects of themselves that in the rush for commercial breaks would be overlooked.

The moral is that too often we neglect the value of unbidden gifts as a way of denigrating both ourselves and the giver. In other words, we feel that we are of so little value that the gift, too, is useless. Or we inflate our "face" value in order to compensate for our own genuine lack of understanding.

For thousands of years, the giving of gifts, especially *unbidden* gifts, was a symbol of feeling and honesty within any relationship. We still talk about the importance of "gifts from the heart," but the most important thing about *any* gift is that it shows an interest in another person, no matter what form that gift takes. Therefore, it is important in any atmosphere of, often, tense social interactions that we may find ourselves in, to be open and aware of these gifts, and allow ourselves the sensitivity to see them.

In social situation with strangers, these subtle, unbidden gifts can include that:

He's looking at you and showing interest in you.

He is giving you his complete attention.

He's made a move toward you, or allowed you to approach him, intentionally welcoming that move.

He is showing you something of himself that allows him to appear vulnerable. He may be shy, stammering, finding it hard to talk to you but he is making the effort. He is nervous in front of you and this, in itself, is a gift. He is overcoming his own difficulties and reticence to speak to you.

He is offering you his phone number, a drink, a seat, or anything that "comes across" from his side of the situation (or territory) to yours.

He is showing you courtesy, warmth, and a real offering of himself, in the midst of what is often a very *unreal*, rushed, or difficult social setting.

Here again, we have that wonderful "crisis" mode that jumps into social settings: a noisy bar; the strained "now-or-never" demands of street meetings—those times when you blank out and regret every second afterward; or the pull of your friends and buddies, when you really want a moment alone with him. All of these things add up to a momentary crisis, but the unbidden gift itself comes in to calm the situation and add a promise of real intimacy, if you recognize it.

Just as you can recognize unbidden gifts, you can also *offer* them. And with an understanding of the importance and role of valor, you can *value* yourself enough to make the first move. You are in control. You will wield the situation.

Some Unbidden Gifts You Offer:

Smile and introduce yourself with your name. Ask him his name, and listen to him while he says it. Say, "It's nice to meet you, John," or whatever his name may be. Most people like hearing their names, especially in a situation where they feel alone and ignored—and we've all been there.

If he is standing, ask him to sit down with you. An unbidden gift is to show that you want someone to be close to you. You're inviting closeness. You are not going into the juvenile idiocy of acting "cool," you're going into the adult control of acting *warm*.

Show patience. This has often been one of my problems. I expect people to open up as quickly as I do. As a writer who's verbally comfortable, I find talking fairly easy. Not everyone does. On the other hand, be patient if he spills out too much talk at first. His nerves are showing.

Make an effort to put him at ease by showing your own vulnerability, as in: "Funny, I've just run out of anything to say. But I'm glad you're here."

Say something about him that you find pleasing or complimentary: "I like your (eyes, smile, voice, shirt . . .)." If he seems flustered or embarrassed, smile. But don't make him feel that you are laughing at him. The truth is few men today receive compliments, because so many people never take the effort to notice them. But you will notice him.

Try to be aware of his breathing (is it rapid or tense?) and other signs that he is not relaxed. Your reserve of valor allows you to offer him some security and relaxation. Touch him in a reassuring way, on his shoulder, arm, or hands. Human touch is comforting. Nowadays, we perceive almost any kind of touch as a potentially threatening, take-no-prisoners come-on, instead of an invitation to a deeper, more satisfying closeness. If he draws away, don't feel rejected. Habits of touching and responding to touch may be undeveloped in him. And there are some men who simply recoil from any form of casual touch. This has nothing to do with you, but their own perceptions of being touched, and also their own history of being touched. They may have been abused as kids, by other boys, men, or adults; they may feel that any form of touching is inappropriate in a public or even semi-public setting. This can come from their home culture growing up, or their perception of this culture.

This is sad, because most men still have a genuine hunger to be touched in a warm, kind, and assuring way.

WORK FOR YOU: Do you remember any unbidden gifts given to you? Can you feel the magic of them, the sense of delight and surprise? If you have "outgrown" any reaction to them, try to reconnect with that feeling of warmth and reconnection to a younger, less hardened self. Now, can you remember unbidden gifts that you have offered to someone? If for any reason you cannot, can you think of times when such an offering would have worked a lot of wonder into a situation?

WORK SPACE:

_____

_____

_____

_____

_____

_____

_____

_____

_____

_____

12 Swimming in Cold Water: Letting Go of Valor, After Inviting It

"Accent-tchu-ate the positive,
E-lim-my-nate the negative.
Latch on to the affirmative.
Don't mess with Mister In-between."

Johnny Mercer

In the next two chapters, I will give you two very helpful thought-pictures for developing that important attitude of valor I've been talking about.

First, the idea of swimming in cold water. To many people the picture of an ocean of cold water is frightening, scary, dark, and dangerous. The image of it can bring on a nightmarish association with drowning. We are afraid that cold water will rob us of what little body warmth we have: something many of us are used to rationing like misers. We also fear that it will expose us as being smaller, shriveling, shivering, and very frightened. (Some of us might remember that feeling of being plunged suddenly into a freezing-cold shower and how scary, even humiliating, it felt.)

So, consciously, we may choose only to swim in warm tropical resort waters, avoiding water closer to home unless it's for a few weeks in late-summer.

This brings to me a revoltingly stupid ad for the U.S. Army that says, "Pain is weakness leaving the body." This is truly Madison Avenue idiocy at its worst.

Pain is your body's natural indicator of stress or injury. Ignoring it can be fatal. In Madison Avenue's view, you can be sold anything if they appeal to the insecure child within; therefore, your own reactions to yourself should be either ignored or denigrated with insults.

On the contrary, being aware of your own pain and that of others is an important part of valor, as long as you realize that you have enough strength and resources within you not to ignore pain but to respond to it; not to let your own fears and associations with cold water keep you from it, but to engage it.

Therefore, you *can* swim in cold water in order to reach someone else. In fact, you can pull him *out* of that cold water if need be, if you feel that is what is necessary. So, symbolically, you may find yourself in that situation of "swimming in cold water"—socially, sexually, or psychologically—with someone. The cold water can be a forbidding social situation, a situation where you feel sexually inadequate or threatened, or even a situation where physical danger is threatened. If you feel that the stakes are worth it, and the someone in question is in danger, even from himself, your own sense of valor can help you go in and do what is necessary to approach him, be with him, and help him.

On the other hand—suppose he simply does not want to be pulled out of cold water? *Ever.* Or he only wants to swim alone? Then it may be just as valorous of you to let go, without denigrating him, until the situation changes. This can produce what I call the Valor of Walking Away.

OK. You've been strong enough and have valued your own needs and desires enough to enter a situation, to open yourself up, and to experience someone else. And you've realized that, after giving it not only your best shot, but a large number of them as well, *he* is simply not in a position to value you. He is, in fact, giving you a large number of signals telling you to fuck off. For whatever reason, this is just *not* going to happen.

How do you feel now? And what can you do to make yourself feel better, to see the situation as something other than devaluing and deflating?

It's here that you need to re-enter that important, very adult self (the one that I've been working on with you), to see that you are still large enough (and intact enough) to leave. You don't have to keep on clinging to a bad situation. You've allowed someone else into your heart, and have tried to open up a passage from him to you, a passage that most of the time will be closed to him. Valorously, you opened it. You should feel good about that. Give yourself some space and time to experience your own *value* at work, and also to "recoup your losses" from the emotional wear and tear that have resulted.

You have been strong enough to risk hurt. That idea should be affirming to you, and bring you back to your own sense of goodness and justice for yourself. Too many men come down hard on themselves any moment they feel rejection. But you need to seek justice for yourself, too, and know that you deserve it. Every bit of it.

Therefore, it's important to see valor as a *component* of your personality, but not the whole of it. You can invite the Knight of Valor in, but don't let him take over completely. Valor can be protective, guiding your heart through those troublesome cold waters, but it can't be a substitute for your heart. It can be the muscle behind your conscience, but not a window dummy for it. It can help you deal with pain, but not completely disperse it.

I am just glad that we have this wonderful ally for ourselves, and it is ours if we know how to find and use it.

WORH FOR YOU: Can you think of a specific time when you needed to walk away, and didn't? Can you imagine now walking away with your own sense of self-worth intact? Be specific about the incident, and feel that self-worth at work.

WORH SPACE:

_____

_____

_____

_____

_____

_____

_____

_____

_____

13 Dunk or Duck:
More Ways to See Yourself at Work

The second thought-picture deals with sports. In any sport, there's a point when the ball is coming right to you and you have a choice: go for it, or duck.

Coaches call this "committing to the ball."

In other words, don't duck!

So, using that important sense of valor, you've gone over to him. You've opened up the conversation and gone from "Hi!" to "It's really crowded here." Then on to a compliment, or a more generalized question and heard what he's had to say.

Now it's time to bring things a little closer to you.

You can offer to get him a drink, or offer to have him sit down with you. Either way, you're committing to him, and suggesting that he commit to you, even if it is in a fairly casual way. As I have said, don't pounce. Give him enough space so that if he wants to walk away, he can do so without confrontation. You want to show enough commitment to indicate that you *are* interested in him (and hopefully vice versa), but no one is marrying anyone at the moment. This tactic also makes it easier for you both to re-enter the situation at some point when his own sense of territory is not so threatened: remember men and that all-important sense of territory!

The drink thing should not be "If I buy you a drink, I have you for the night," but simply a good-natured offering. One of the best ways to do this is by observing, "It looks like you are ready for another."

If he says, "No," then say, "How about a soda?"

It may be that he simply does not want to drink any more alcohol, which is understandable. Some men find meeting anyone for the first time unnerving, and they want to have all their wits about them when it happens.

If he refuses either offer, don't worry about it. It may be that he's not ready for what's going on, but might be a short time later. Like I said, in our stranger-phobic society, any kind of interaction threatens even the most secure-looking men. They are sure that you are Osama Bin Laden's cousin, just by the fact that you've walked over to them.

That is their problem, but it shouldn't be yours.

What you're doing is following enough of a script to be comfortable with what's going on, and for him to feel comfortable, too. One of the hallmarks of the art of seduction, as opposed to the old games of hard-core cruising, desperate bar pickups, or whatever you want to term them, is that any form of put-down is not a part of this. Instead, you want to create a field where *both* of you feel good.

So, now is the time for a little self-revelation, but make it general enough that he does not feel that you're revealing all the family secrets. I'll go into the why of this soon.

"I always think it's hard speaking to strangers, don't you?" (This shows that this is an effort for you, too. You're not a professional at this, and you're quite human. So do the next revelations.)

"I'm not much for drinking myself."

"Sometimes I feel that no one is really interested in talking to anybody. I wonder why?"

"The hard thing is figuring out what you want to say, after you find someone you think you want to talk to. Do you have that problem?"

You may have other revelations of your own, if you think about it. What you're doing is offering him a small insight into your personality and giving him an opportunity to reveal something about himself.

That is very important. Most people are flattered that you're interested in them, even if they can't come back with an answer to your questions. So the fact that you cared enough to ask will *normally* please them.

But some men are simply socially impaired. You've probably met a couple yourself. Any attempt to meet them, know them, even please them, is met with either frosty aloofness or hostility. Their level of self-contempt and contempt for others is so high, and so ingrained, that they are suspicious of natural kindness.

Don't let men like this bother you. Whatever has brought them to this point is not your affair, or problem. When they go on "auto-bitch," don't let that bother you either. Meeting people *is* natural, and meeting this type of guy is too, I'm afraid. I've found with many men like this that at some point they realize what they've missed, and exactly whose fault it is, and at that point they are genuinely sad.

Another situation that should be talked about is that he may simply be taking time to get his bearings about you. He may be curious, interested, and actually glad that you've made this move toward him, but not be registering much. He may even seem stony or icy to you. In this case, provide a little more space between you. Step back a foot or so. Keep smiling, but don't feel that you're being reduced to a window manikin because you have no idea what to do next. The truth is that you have decided to give him more space and time, and you are secure enough not to feel awkward about doing it. If after enough time you feel that this is going nowhere, then say: "It's been nice speaking with you. Maybe we can talk again at some point."

A Note About Revelations

Too many, too personal self-revelations make you appear desperate, lonely, and even superficial. You've just met this guy and already you're telling him about your miserable childhood, your deepest traumas, your most pathetic hang-ups, and whatever's left after that.

Several years ago I met a man at a party—we were casually thrown together—and within five minutes, he told me: "I have to tell you, I'm an incest survivor." We were standing up with drinks in our hands. He then went into who'd done it, when, and how.

I was floored. Such a level of trust he seemed to have in . . . little ol' me? Whatever seductive charms I had must have been working overtime.

About ten minutes later, we parted. He went back to whomever he was with and I did the same. Two weeks later, at another event, I ran into the same gentleman. I went up to him, smiled, and he said to me, "Have we ever met?"

Moral of this story: Don't do that.

If you spill *all* of your beans, you get to keep none for yourself and the beans mean nothing. We live in an era of messy, easy, cheapened confessions that destroy genuine intimacy. This is one of the reasons why seduction has become such a lost art form. So, in the beginning, let him see some of you, but keep most of it to yourself. You'll both be happier that way.

14 Three Necessities One Should *Not* Leave Home Without

"Ah yes, Love . . . Love, at the moment, was J."
Christopher Isherwood, *Prater Violet*

OK. To use a more ancient form of technology, we're going to rewind a bit here and get you back to that point where you're either still standing close or sitting next to each other. Most important, you've established the fact that you're interested in him. This should be the basic foundation of everything: that *you* (valorously!) have made this move. You've done what you wanted to do, what you set out to do, and what you are now doing. Having established this, now is *not* the time to "take this to the next level" as they say in the world of high-pressure salesmanship, but to allow him to have a moment to see how really nice you are.

The fact is, you're *not* here to show him how blindingly bright you are. How drop-dead glammy you are. How smart and successful you are (in fact, how so much above him you are that he'll have to strain like hell to reach you). You're showing him that you are interested in him, and sharing some of your own time and genuine niceness with him.

These are pretty old-fashioned values, and I'm sure that many politicians would love to be able to do this, but can't. The truth is, you don't want his vote, you just want to enjoy the fact that he's there *close* to you.

This is the time to come out with three really important things you should never leave home without—and I don't mean lube, rubbers, and a pair of handcuffs.

I mean your own interest in the following *three* topics:
1) "What kind of work do you do?"
2) "Do you have other things that you are really crazy about?"
3) "Have you seen any movies or things lately that you liked?"

To Elaborate:

"What kind of work do you do?" is one of the most important questions you can ask anyone, but men especially warm up to it. It does not mean how important are you, and how much money do you make, but it asks what is it that you do that occupies a very important part of your day. And note: I also don't ask "What do you do for a living?" Many men do not *work* for a living, for whatever reason, but they do have work that they do.

Men, in general, love to talk about their work—either as something they love or hate, but definitely as something that's important to them. One of the worst mistakes you can make with a man is to say, "Don't tell me about your work, tell me about the *real* you."

For most men, the "real you" is their work. It's a very important part of their lives, and without it they are missing that center that most of life spins around.

So, once he answers, be interested in it. I have found that as I get older, most people's jobs become more interesting to me—and ones I'd never do myself, that seem so completely outside my own sphere of behavior and abilities, are the *most* interesting.

Years ago, I met a gay undertaker, something I could not imagine myself doing—and realized I was fascinated that he dealt with people under some of the most difficult circumstances in their lives. If I'd met him at twenty-three, I might have run away from him as fast as I could. A gay undertaker! But at forty-three I was enthralled. This revealed to me that one sign of maturity is that very little people do stays *un*interesting once you understand its place in human life.

So, be interested in what he does, even if only to say, "I don't know anything about that. What's that like?"

Then proceed to the second really important question.

Asking "Do you have other things that you're really crazy about?" gives him a chance to talk about other things that mean something to him. Hobbies, passions, obsessions. If he clams up here, don't worry. This does not mean he's suddenly rejecting you. Like so many people, he may not know how to respond. Don't make him feel that you're prying. You're just interested. You can say, "I don't really have a lot of time for other things myself, but I do have a dog, car, apartment I've redecorated six times . . . and I like drives in the country, going to the beach when I can; I am fascinated by the lives of others, read the newspaper from cover to cover, spend a lot of time online, eat out three times a week."

Tell him something about yourself, but don't make it so personal that he feels intimidated by it.

There's a reason for not getting too personal. If you get too personal, he may feel that he can't reveal something quite so intimate about himself and therefore he's already "lost" the game. You don't want this to happen. The important thing is to make sure that you both stay in the game.

After all, you've already committed to the ball.

There's one "caveat" (a warning!) about delving into a man's profession. Some men have professions that are confidential and secret. He may work for the CIA, the FBI, or be a private bodyguard to Steve Gates (I actually met someone like that once). There may be cases where he's not going to let you in to a lot of his professional life, so don't pry if he shuts the door nicely with "I can't tell you any more."

But if he *slams* the door with "That's none of your business," then you have a decision to make.

You can apologize and say, "Sorry. I didn't mean to pry." Then you can smile, and watch for clues from him. Does he realize how boorish his behavior is? Is he apologizing for acting like an asshole?

Or, is he indicating, very frankly, that he really doesn't want to go any further with you?

If you feel that his behavior is really not in keeping with what you want, then it is perfectly fair to say, "I'm sorry. Maybe this is not something we should be doing."

Seduction does not mean being a *doormat*. Always keep that in mind.

However, some men have jobs that they are not going to share very much of with you. It's as simple as that. But they should be flattered that you are interested in what they do.

Finally, we come to, "Have you seen any movies or things lately that you liked?" Variations on this are, "Read any good books lately?" "Did you see that last episode of *Lost*?" Or, "Have you been to [whatever attraction is popular in your area at this time, a museum show, a beach, a gay expo, anything that he might have attended or you just did]?"

Again, basically what you're establishing is a sense of nonthreatening interest, but also one that is becoming warmer. You show this by continuing to have fairly regular eye contact with him, as well as smiling. Your body language is showing him that you are going further than the talk is showing, and getting ready for your next move, which will be closer, and more intimate.

Here you should also understand three basics that are going on, along with the three essentials that you have brought out:

1) You are sharing territory with him. Men are territorial, and the fact that he has allowed you into his territory, just as you have with good intentions moved into his territory, is very important. A lot of people

forget this in the difficulties of "icebreaking," or starting a "real" conversation.

2) Therefore, any conversation he has with you is important because *he* is having it. Understanding this requires some maturity and sophistication on your part. The fact that you may not agree on everything is not nearly as important as the fact that you are both still talking.

3) Your listening to him is a gift that you are giving him, just as what he is saying to you is a gift. I know with myself since I am an attentive listener that it takes some energy to listen to people, therefore I see listening as an important part of any conversation. So don't feel that if you've run out of words the "game" is up. Smiling, looking into his eyes and face, and any form of light, casual touching keeps your presence very much with him.

WORK FOR YOU: Think of something about yourself that you'd like to share with someone (a recent experience or activity), and also how you'd like to bring another man's experiences into it: Perhaps he has done the same thing, or even the opposite. Perhaps he has never done anything like it, and you can explain its attractions. Enthusiasm is contagious, but keep it low-keyed enough so that it opens a door rather than hits him directly in the face.

WORK SPACE:

_____

_____

_____

_____

_____

_____

_____

_____

15

Approaching the Physical Moves; or Practice, Practice, Practice

"Some day he'll come along, / The man I love; /
And he'll be big and strong, / The man I love."
Ira Gershwin

Although I've spoken somewhat about the physical aspects of what's going on (positioning, his placement, yours), we both have to admit that most of this so far has been pretty cerebral. That is, I've been asking you to do your inner homework, giving you a lot of theory and framework, and trying to get you to work through in your head what, later, your body will be doing.

So, there's *theory* here, with very few nitty-gritty nuts and bolts.

Speaking for myself, I like the nitty-gritty and the nuts and bolts a lot, but I know you have to be prepared with a "head plan" before you know how to use them. The truth is, the Art of Seduction (like dance, jazz, bowling, diving, wrestling, cooking, screwing, and other art forms) is very physical. It's *visceral*. It comes right out of your gut. And although I'm trying to give you a sense of choreography (so you're not out there all by yourself without a plan with which to make your next move), much of it depends on physical responses and how well you do them, as well as how good you are at controlling your own re-sponses—especially the famous "flight or fight" response that makes you want to pack up and run as soon as you feel any threatening hint of non-interest or rejection.

And, I know this *is* threatening.

I've known many good and smart men who could approach an en-emy in the field with a bayonet, but could not approach a stranger in a bar. I've also known bona fide nitwits who are very good at this.

What makes them good?

Practice.

As with any real art form, practice does not always make perfect, but it does allow you to approach perfection when you need to. The problem is that a lot of guys don't know this, and they feel that when the right man does come along (as in the song, "Some day he'll come along / the man I love"), they will automatically know how to behave.

He does, and they don't.

In fact, he might have come many times, and they still didn't. (You can use the term "come" here in as many meanings of the term as you want. But they *still* didn't know!)

So, unless you've got the perfect fairy godmother guiding you (and you probably don't), practicing beforehand is a good idea.

Here are some things to practice.

Smiling. I know, you're thinking, I need to practice smiling like Bugs Bunny needs to practice munching carrots. But the right smile can make a huge difference. Never make a man feel that you are smiling at his expense, that the joke is on him and you are smiling out of defensiveness. He has got to see that you're smiling because you *like* what you see, and you're *sincerely* interested in him.

So, the big, nervous, laugh-at-you smile is out.

Now, in your mirror, practice smiling so that your eyes smile more than your mouth. Part of this can be achieved by not staring directly at him when you're looking at him (no "cruise-of-death" eyeballs here, please!), but look at the *light* around him and allow yourself to smile because of that light. In other words, you are smiling because you're looking at the glow around him, not directly at him.

What we want is a nice, slightly open, winning, affectionate, sincere smile. None of that "GOD ALMIGHTY!!!! I just won MISS AMERICA!!!!" full-beam-headlights clown-face grin, please.

You want your eyes to be in view, your mouth slightly turned up. It's a Mona Lisa, Bette Davis, Clint Eastwood, Gary Cooper, Cary Grant, who-can-resist-it? kind of smile, the smile that Leonardo da Vinci captured, just like any decent, hard-working, overpaid Hollywood movie star who didn't want to wrinkle his/her face up so much that those gorgeous light-capturing eyes didn't show.

Because the truth is you want to capture the light in *his* eyes with yours, and with your smile.

So practice this. Know what it looks like, and what it feels like. If you have access to a video camera, video it so that you can see what it looks like. This kind of seductive smile is a hard thing to practice with your friends, and I strongly suggest not trying it on a bus or other any other form of public transport, although strangely enough children do it all the time with one another—and with adults, too.

Children early on are naturally seductive, and you probably remember smiling that way at someone at school without even knowing you were trying to seduce him (or her). The truth is, seduction is something that is natural to people, and we try very hard to erase it. We try to deny it because the results are too threatening, even when they're fairly innocent. Popular kids at school are constantly seductive. The question is, how far will they go with their seductiveness?

I was lucky when I was a kid, because my favorite aunt showed me by example how to smile seductively. Aunt Louise looked like a dead-ringer for Greta Garbo: perfect cheekbones, classic features, and naturally springy, glossy blonde hair that swung beautifully every time she tossed her head. She was very much aware of this, and had this way of smiling so that her eyes smiled and her mouth just lifted slightly at the corners. It was mysterious, inviting, and irresistible. She was also from the Deep South, like I am, where seduction is such a natural pastime that you become used to it. You hardly suspect it; it seems like an organic part of life.

This of course made me a naturally seductive child, and by the time I was in my mid-teens I realized that I could get what I wanted through charm and seduction. Like many other people who learn this early, I realized these were very useful skills, although they can only get you so far. But at certain times, far enough.

The other thing to practice is looking someone in the eye. In our culture, looking anyone in the eye has become extremely threatening, and there are individuals who can become violent because of it. This is sad, because in many other cultures and times, not being able to look someone in the eye was considered an indication of dishonesty. Nowadays, we wonder why you're doing it, and try to judge the level of threat when it's done.

The point is to look someone in the eye, but not stare. Don't use this as a form of aggression—of showing, "Look, I can do this!"—but as a form of invitation, meaning, "I want to invite you closer to me."

One way to produce this softer eye contact is to look at someone from an angle, rather than straight on. Cock your head slightly while looking. When you do this while presenting that smile-with-your-eyes smile you've been practicing, it's inviting without being threatening, alluring without being saccharine.

You should also learn to synchronize the smile and the eye contact while you're doing the opening talk. For some men, this may be difficult. They are too nervous to smile and talk at the same time, too afraid they're going to forget what they feel they *have* to say. And they're afraid they're going to come off like fools.

Remember this. In fact, commit it to memory: *slight nervousness can be alluring, too.*

That's right. A slight tang of nerves, a show that you are not completely smooth, can put you on the same level that he is, and it is, most of the time, delightful. Jimmy Stewart kept that little boyish stutter. He could have got rid of it, but it made him appealing. I adore shy men because I started out as one, and deep inside am still very shy. So, don't be afraid of your nervousness, but realize it is a part of your innate charm and can be exquisitely seductive. And if this very nervousness keeps your smile, eye contact, and words from happening all at the same time, don't worry. If you need to, close your eyes for a moment, then experience bringing him back in again with them.

WORK FOR YOU: Spend some time at the mirror looking at the way you smile. Is it forced? Is it too "hard"? Is it the kind of "salesman's smile" you can see through at once? Now, stop smiling for a moment, close your eyes, and think of something extremely pleasant—a vacation on a tropical beach, a wonderful meal you remember, a point in your childhood you loved. Open your eyes and look at your smile. Is it the same smile? It shouldn't be. Try to hold and feel how soft and inviting that new smile is. Practice this smile several times; do it over several days. Now realize that you can smile this way when you want to.

WORK SPACE:

Give me three memories or ideas that produce
a pleasant smile in you—

_____

_____

_____

_____

_____

16 Getting Back to Touch

"Dart took every opportunity he could find to bump into Brad—preferably underwater—and learn more about his body."

Aaron Krach, *Half-Life*

For some men touching is so difficult that they're sure their hands are going to catch fire the moment they attempt it. In the beginning, they can do the smile, and maybe, if they work it, some eye contact. But actually touching a stranger is still horrifying to them.

This is our touch-phobic, stranger-phobic culture hard at work. It's difficult to say where all this touch-phobia began, but it is now so in place, so constant, that many of us spend our lives not touching anything. That means we don't touch any physical, inanimate, or (God forbid!) living thing. Even touching pets is scary for some people.

In fact, most of the time during your day, you have to buy it *before* you can touch it.

The old-fashioned five-and-dime stores and farmers markets where all sorts of goods and merchandise were displayed openly for customers to handle are close to gone. Now everything is enclosed in sealed, theft-proof plastic bubbles. No touching allowed. Meat, fish, and vegetables are all plastic-wrapped in supermarkets. I remember getting into a fight once because I sniffed a fresh tomato. A fellow shopper was appalled. I told her, "You do wash it, once you get it home, don't you?"

In contemporary culture, most men no longer shake hands, except very guardedly, or touch each other on the shoulder, or hug, or share any physical intimacy unless under very specific circumstances. (It may be permitted briefly at funerals; and that's it!) The Woodstock generation is close to dead; now we have the Wal-Mart generation. So you can see that touching is very difficult.

It's also extremely welcome and necessary.

Why is that so?

One reason is that touching is a basic human want, especially among men. A famous study done twenty-odd years ago on children found that young boys really want to be touched and hugged as a form of reward and recognition, while girls, as their form of recognition, want to be praised. Girls want to be told that they are pretty, smart, and special. Boys want to be shown that they are worthy of affection. So turning a cold shoulder to them hurts them. Yet we starve boys of physical affection from the time they are five or six, and often stop praising little girls because we're sure it embarrasses them.

This is one reason why boys love contact sports like football and wrestling; but any team sport can afford great touching opportunities, either from winning, as in group hugs, or in losing, as in more group hugs.

So, although men innately love and desire touching, all this touch-fear around us brings up the difficult questions. When do I do it, and how?

First realize this: You *can* seduce without touching. But touching is an excellent, high-end-luxury express train to it.

And even a guy who recoils at your touch, from learned reflex, may be enjoying it inside.

Touching creates this connection between you that is electric, and is closely connected to your own valorous center, that center of bravery, confidence, and warmth.

Touching is an energy force, and you are giving him some of your own personal warmth and feelings, your own good energy. I have met dozens of amazingly good-looking guys who've told me that they cannot get a date, they never meet anyone, they bomb out every night—and I've noticed, right off the bat, that they're incapable of touching. It's like there's this invisible but noticeable shield around them, and they cannot reach out of it. For so long they've had hammered into them that touching is "not appropriate." It's out of bounds, "unprofessional." It can get them into trouble. It means they're "sexually compulsive." And it is definitely a clue to a "character flaw."

It worked that way with Bill Clinton, who was a famous "toucher," and who still loves to hug and shake hands with everyone. The word on the street is, "Watch out! Look what it did for Bill! It brought him Monica, with Ken Starr on his tail!"

One of the few bright lights around in this area is Barack Obama, who is a wonderful toucher. So maybe touching will make a come back.

I'm afraid touching has become as much an indication of deviousness and underhanded evil as keeping three black cats and a box of toads in your room. You are "innocent," until you start touching. There are even those omnipresent surveillance video cameras set up to catch you doing it.

But no matter how paranoid we've become, men for the most part still love to touch and be touched. And for too many of them, it's something they don't do. This lack of touching has left them feeling completely alone.

Alone physically, emotionally— and very much, sexually.

This is tragic, because touching is an innate human need. And in many other cultures, other than our own hard-core competitive, back-to-Puritanism one, it is looked upon benignly and graciously. Italian men touch all over the place; Arab men openly hold hands and nuzzle; Russian men whisper into each other's ear; French men kiss each other on the cheek; and in New Guinea, naked men calmly hold each other's penises. You don't have to be a rocket scientist to figure it out. Guys like to touch and be touched, and derive a genuine sense of closeness from it.

But *we* don't do it.

So being able to explore and offer touching puts you into a very good category. It means that you are initiating warmth that is necessary, though often not available. Keeping this in mind, begin your own touching exercises. That is, get used to being touched and to touching.

Touching Exercises

In a social situation (as opposed to a private, sexual one), what places do you feel good about being touched? Hands? Arms? Face? Neck? Shoulders? Chest?

As a beginning exercise, allow yourself a moment alone, with no distractions. Before your mirror, touch your own face slowly, gliding with the palm of your hand. Now do it with your fingers, one at a time, then together, carefully, slowly. You'll find that each of your fingers feels differently touching your face. It also matters if you've shaved recently, or have stubble. Close your eyes and do it, and then open your eyes again, and do it some more.

Now touch your neck, the back of it, and then your throat. Close your eyes and imagine being touched there. Use your fingertips as if they are traveling very slowly over the terrain of this part of your body.

Now, touch your chest, very, very slowly. You can do this clothed, and then do it unclothed. You can also do it in the shower, before going to sleep, or when waking up. Men who have no problems masturbating often forget that there are other places to touch themselves, and these places are really hungering to be touched.

Now, still alone, but you don't have to be in front of your mirror, touch your own hands. Let your fingers interact with each other. Touch the backs of your hands. Feel the hair there, the smooth places, the way that the wrist gives way to the back of the hand, then to the fingers. Fingers are extremely sensitive things, and most of us use them either locked together, as if they are enclosed in mittens, or like tense grips waiting to latch on to something. Now, touch your arms, the upper arm, the forearms, and the wonderfully sensitive places at the elbow and inside the crook of the elbow.

Men who like to receive massages often have less trouble touching other men, but this is not always true. So, alone, start massaging yourself, too, using your full hand (all fingers go!), as well as lighter pressure from just your fingertips. Massage your neck and shoulders, your upper arms and legs, as well as places on your chest. You may start to notice how much tension there is in these places, even with you doing the massaging. This tension is resolved a lot faster if someone else is doing it (it is a little harder to massage yourself and unwind) but even doing it yourself, you can feel some of the tension unlocking.

You'll also begin to see how wonderful touch is. And just how much you've really been missing it.

If you find that you've been locked into this touch-phobic world so badly that you had no idea how much you'd been missing until you read this, one way to get out of it is to join a gay men's massage group, or form one of your own. There are massage groups all over the country in larger cities, and networks of men into these groups. One of the largest networks is Body Electric, which runs schools and workshops about massage. One warning: A lot of men who are Body Electric graduates still cannot practice touch as a means of seduction. It is still difficult for them to place touch within an emotionally-inviting context.

So it's now time to do this. It's now time to venture into your first seductive touch.

WORK FOR YOU: Do not stop practicing touching. You can do it at night before going to sleep. Allow yourself a moment at lunch to do it, or do it any time you want to reward yourself. This kind of touching intimacy with yourself, that you will later use with another person, is private. You don't have to explain it or rationalize it. It's for the pure pleasure of doing it.

17

Everyman's Land.
That First Delicious Touch

"In the stillness in the autumn moonbeams his
face was inclined toward me,
And his arm lay lightly around my breast—
and that night I was happy."

Walt Whitman,
"When I Heard at the Close of the Day"

I want to take touching out of the Land of Theory and into the Land of Reality. How you will arrange this will be up to you and your own circumstances with other men. But the next time you are in a potentially seductive situation with another man, realize that one of the best places to start a seductive touch is under his arm, slightly below his armpit—as if you are drawing him closer to you.

Looking into his eyes (but not staring), place your hand very gently there, and exert the smallest degree of pressure you can. Some men will tense up as an ingrained social reflex, but if you keep your hand there, relaxed for a moment, they will relax. This also brings you closer to him, and it means that you can lower your voice to a more intimate level. If the two of you are still talking about things that are fairly general, it means that no matter where the conversation is going, it's now serving two purposes:

1) It's allowing what talk does: communicating something. This means that no matter what is being said (it can be about the Yankees, the economy, jobs, the price of tea in China, etc.) there is the intention to communicate, and *that* is what is important. So don't worry about making points or trying to outwit anyone.

2) It means that the two of you are close enough, and not going anywhere. Establishing this in itself is the most important aspect of communication at this point.

You may find that he really likes this, and is comfortable being touched by you in this warm, unthreatening way. You're now less than an arm's length from him, and for some men this is a real revelation too. Many of us are so used to distant, generalized, cocktail party chatter that the mere fact that you have placed yourself within another man's physical space changes everything. It may mean to him that you are authentically interested in him, and this in itself, after so much counterfeit interest, is important.

On the other hand, some men still have problems with physical touching. They are not comfortable with it, especially in a situation that is at all public. For them, the physical touch becomes too aligned with a threat. This threat may now take the form that you are "coming on" to him and twenty-odd years of training may be warning him: "What's going on here? This is dangerous territory!"

If you do feel him becoming tense or "uptight" about what you're doing, don't freak out yourself, or revert to being "cool." His reaction does not necessarily mean rejection; it just means that all of our touch-phobic training is at work. So stay in control, and *warm*. Draw back a bit. You might remove your hand from him, but not yourself. Continue smiling in that warm, soft, and engaging way that you practiced. Let him continue to feel that he does have some space of his own. (Remember the importance of male territorialism.) He may be wondering what's going on, which is fine—it just shows you that an amazing number of guys still have to be hit over the head with a shovel. They can't figure out that you're sexually interested in them—because most of their "sex" is now online, and a huge amount of it is done alone.

Online sex, all by itself, has turned seduction into a close-to-lost art form. So as a master of it, you're in a very good place. At a certain point you'll be able to gauge (and gear) your own activities to what's going on, so the fact that you're comfortable with this means that *you* are now in control.

Here is where valor comes into play. No matter what happens—even if he runs screaming from the room (worst case scenario!)—you are still the one who knows what's going on, and how to use it.

You little devil! Who'd think you'd be able to go so *far* in so little time? Doesn't it feel great?

If he is still there, after the hand under his arm, try brushing the back of your fingers very lightly, and briefly, on his cheek—exactly as you have practiced doing this on yourself at home. Or, casually bring your fingers to the side of his neck and let them simply drift down for a moment. Smile while you do this, and get close enough to him that you are both breathing within the same space. At this point, exhale softly and relax.

Let him feel that you are completely relaxed doing this, and he should be too.

Here I need to inject a bit of advice about space, especially *male* space.

Men, as I have said, are territorial animals; but what their space means has nothing to do with the size of the territory as much as the fact that they feel in control in it (and sometimes *of* it). Therefore a lot of the rejection vibes we feel coming from men is not an actual rejection as it is a reaffirmation of their need for a safe space. This space can be totally psychological. If he feels that you are injecting yourself and your opinions too hard, too forcefully, on him, then his psychological space is being threatened and he will either retract from you, or become defensive. His reaction may come from all sorts of ingrained feelings, psychological and emotional situations (or just plain "baggage"), and the way he feels that his own character has been formed and expresses itself. He may feel "offended" by you getting closer to him, even though, in truth, he may already actually like you.

We, therefore, have potentially working what I would call, to put it in plain English, the "asshole imperative." Don't be one, or force him to become one. In other words, don't draw away from him, either physically or verbally, so fast that he feels you are using your proximity as something you can instantly retract and hurt him with. This is often the case when a would-be seducer uses ploys like put-downs to impress a man, or worse, to make him feel rejected. Even your putting down other men in the room can make him feel defensive, as he perceives that he can easily be your next target. So, I know what a clever, bright person you are, but keep it to yourself now.

It can also be that the setting of your initial contact, no matter where it is, doesn't relax him. If it is in a public or even semi-public place, such as the corner of a bar, a club, or whatever, he feels that "people are watching," and this is a kind of intimacy between two men that cannot be public in any way. There are still a lot of guys, especially young men, in our Age of the New Victorianism (all of the old repression, without those really interesting clothes!) who firmly believe in not "scaring the horses." (You might remember Queen Victoria saying that it did not matter what you did, as long as "You do not scare the horses.")

Anyway, there are men out there like this (I call them "decorum boys"), and you never can tell when you're going to meet one. One thing that always amazes me about these lads is that although they may be unnerved by any show of affection or feelings in public, they often are the ones blabbing to the whole world on their cell phones about things that would make any decent whore blush. And they're doing it out loud, out *there*. But go figure. Humans are not famous for consistency.

Therefore, if this man you're being seductive with indicates in any way that this is just too much for him, respect that. It may mean that he needs another moment to get used to it, at which point he will relax, too.

It can also help if you say, in a very intimate tone, something like:

"I wondered what it would be like to do this."

"I think this is nice, being able to touch you."

"This feels really nice."

"What were you saying before, about [movies, books, Fire Island real estate, that famous price of tea in China, etc.]?"

One of the nicer things about touching is that it can automatically put both of you in a win-win situation, by removing huge amounts of the conversational tension and stress from the situation. Because now it really doesn't make that much difference if he cannot come up with the cutest, smartest, brightest comeback in the world, or any comeback for that matter.

You are simply enjoying each other's presence and physicality on a genuinely affectionate level. And even if he decides he does not want any of this, if it's time for him to get up and answer that long waiting e-mail from someone in Nigeria with the $30 million to give him, and he will "see you around," you've still done something that few men have the presence of mind and control to do, and, one way or another, this has brought you further along in your own process of being seductive, whether he has stayed a part of it or not.

In fact, it may be his loss not being a part of it.

You would, in truth, be surprised at how many men painfully recognize the fact that they cannot respond to seduction, and this hurts them. It shows that they are not emotionally connected enough to allow it to happen. They may fantasize a great deal about it (and huge amounts of porn in various forms uses seduction as a basic tool), but when the rubber hits the road, they take off. They cannot deal with something that requires them to be both relaxed and present at the same time. They are missing out on so much satisfaction, and they know it.

At this point, you may be ready for something else. You've offered a couple of cards from your part of the deck, and seen how he responded to them. It may be that you've decided that *he's* the wrong one. After all, you're not kissing him, making out like teenagers (or like they used to—the kids have stopped much of that, too), and you haven't said, "Your place or mine?"

What you've done is shown interest in him, and if you feel that he's just another frog on your way to a prince, then it's not a bad idea to decide right now to call it quits.

However, as I said, don't do it like a heel. Don't slam doors. Because he may have some surprises of his own, like the fact that he's much warmer and more interested in you than he can actually show at the present.

This lack of a quick reaction does bother a lot of men who want to be seductive. They may be employing many of their seductive gifts, only to find that they're falling on deaf ears, blind eyes, and very stiff arms.

They don't understand that a lot of men simply do not understand the art and language of seduction, or will not permit themselves to respond to it. A number of years ago I met a sweetly attractive guy at a gay bar in Provincetown. I was drawn to him, and we started talking. He was from an extremely repressed Polish Catholic family in a working-class town in upstate New York, and totally in the closet. This was his first time in very gay P'town, and even though this was in the early 1990s going there meant, as he told me, "I had to lie to everyone. My mom wanted to know where I was going for my vacation. I couldn't tell her. I couldn't tell anyone at work. My mom always wants to know everything about me, and I can't lie to her because it'll hurt her too much."

He was in his late thirties, and I thought this was really sad. Would he ever grow up and have a life of his own? But he was so attractive that I found myself going into autopilot seduction with him, though he seemed completely unresponsive to it. After a while, he told me he needed to go to the men's room, which I was sure was his excuse to get away and a good time for me to exit as well. The next day I saw him on the beach, and he told me how miserable he was that I'd left, that he had really enjoyed meeting me, giving me every indication that I was not on the wrong track with him.

I could only smile, thinking: I guess this is a lesson for the both of us. Not everyone understands the language of seduction, but a large number of men are interested in being seduced.

The real question is, do they know *how* interested they are? Sometimes they don't, and then it is up to you to make the decision how far to take this, how patient to be with them, and how much time and energy you want to spend pursuing them.

One thing I can definitely say in favor of these men is that once you land them, they are usually worth the effort.

WORK FOR YOU: Make a list of guys you'd like to do these first seductive moves with. The list can include guys you know, guys you've seen in bars or at parties, or even men you've seen briefly on the street. Try to imagine touching them in the ways we've talked about in this chapter. Now, keep a thought-picture in your mind of succeeding with these gestures. Keep that thought-picture until it is time to start doing this in reality. Remember, how soon you go from theory to reality is up to you, but don't procrastinate too long. Like any other activity, it is easy to become out of practice in seduction.

WORK SPACE:
Your List!—

_____

_____

_____

_____

_____

_____

_____

_____

_____

18

CHAPTER

Touching and Beyond: Two Helpful Concepts

Before I go further with touching—and touching is something I like very much—I thought I would share with you two concepts that I think may be helpful to anyone dealing with touch, when to touch, how to break out of touch-phobia, and/or your own reticence or shyness about these matters.

These two concepts fly directly into the face of a lot of the "accepted wisdom" of this period; that is, some of the clichés (and b.s.) making seduction (and truly satisfying living) very difficult.

The first deals with the concept of "issues."

Much of our culture is now dominated by the "culture of business" which will do anything to advance sales, make the office a smooth-running and personality-free environment, and in the process prevent (and/ or gloss over) any truth that is either inconvenient or "uncomfortable."

Therefore, the term "issue" has taken over where the old, very useful word "problem" worked nicely. In short, you don't want to have *problems* now. Problems are presented as accusations, as in: "You got a problem?"

No one wants problems, because problems have to be met, addressed, and solved—or not solved, therefore remaining problems. In a nutshell, problems are bad for business; therefore, in the business world, problems are rarely ever admitted.

Instead, you have *issues*.

The term "issue" originally meant "to come out, to go out." It also referred to children, who were the "issue" (or result of a union) of Jim and Sarah or Punch and Judy. Or that money was the "issue" of planting alfalfa instead of soybeans. How *issue* became a soft-core term for problems, I don't know, but on a personal level, what it has left us with are the "issue guys" who simply never get over their problems.

Their problems remain "issues," that is, difficult situations left over from *real* problems that will never actually be addressed. What I'm saying is, problems you *can* face. You can address them. You can work hard to get over them, and probably will. But issues, well, they are here to stay!

So, back to the touching situation. Some men will tell you they have an "issue" with touching. It goes back to their childhood, to abuse, to social and religious repression. These "issues" they (and you) may not be able to get past. But the actual *problem* of being touched and allowing touch . . . you can face that and even get them over it.

Many "issues" with problems come from the fact that the fear around them makes them difficult to face. You're more afraid of your fear of rejection than of actual rejection. <u>You are more afraid of how people see you than you are aware of what you really look like.</u>

So, many problems can be addressed, and solved, by facing them, or by having help with them. "Issues," though, I'm afraid often do not. The idea of issues is to tiptoe around them, so that not facing them, not solving them, does not prevent the regular "normal" course of business from happening.

While I have seen many men who are traumatized by their problems, they will not really face them as long as they stay "issues." They will simply announce, "I have an issue around meeting men." "I have self-esteem issues." "I have social-phobia issues."

So, my first concept for you is: We don't have "issues," anymore. We have *real* problems. And we can face these problems, at least enough to allow the seductions we want to take place.

The second concept is "self-esteem."

Self-esteem has become one of the watchwords of this current period. Kids now take classes in it, corporations offer workshops in it, and nobody wants not to have it. Self-esteem becomes like a Band-Aid we stick over a basic problem (and here it is a problem, not an "issue") of a lack of a real feeling of self.

Self is that part of you that is permanent, deep, lovely, and real, that so many people are now separated from. Sometimes the self is capitalized, as in the Self, but it is that deep, imaginative aspect of ourselves that as an identifiable entity comes closest to our souls. It is that thing that in a better world your parents would give you as a birthright, that you would see as something innately beautiful, and that operates like a gyro to keep you on an even keel, balanced within nature and within human life.

However, we don't live in that perfect world, so the Self often gets lost. We have a hard time being in contact with it, and when we really do lose it, we descend into depression. Stress can do that, it can produce a continuing battering of your Self; also the loss of people close to you, and a sense of hopelessness that can come from adverse circumstances. These all lead to a genuine loss of *self.* (OK, I'll go back to lower-casing it.)

It is at those moments that you need to recapture that self, and a mere sense of "self-esteem" is not going to work. In previous chapters I have talked about working on having intimacy with yourself. Or, with your self. In these first "essays" or attempts at touching, having that self-intimacy is very important. It gives you not only the support you need to proceed with touching, but also a beautiful and very decent sense of protection. Very vulnerable people do not touch, but sensitive people do. There is a vast difference between the two, and I want to develop in you your own sense of self and your sensitivity to it, without the wounding sense of vulnerability that will keep you from going forth and touching.

And touching is very much a part of "going forth," of extending your own territory, and breaking out of the locked, lonely environment so many of us have constructed around ourselves.

If you feel that you have "self-esteem issues," the real problem is that you've been, for too long, separated from your own, very real self.

One of the ways we know the self is really working is that it allows us to be alone without a sense of loneliness. If you are alone too much, for weeks, months, years on end, then loneliness may become a problem. But many people cannot be alone for any amount of time. They have to be with people they may not really like, but who dispel some of that terrible loneliness. You get this in constant nervous cell phone chatter; in people who have to be e-mailable 24/7 and in people whose lives are now consumed by social networking sites. They cannot be "out of touch" for a second, or their loneliness will come roaring back at them.

This is often true of younger people, but older ones also get caught in this trap. They always have some game, diversion, or entertainment going, instead of finding time for their own thoughts, feelings, reactions, and a genuine *touching* closeness to others.

This has left many men with a terrible vacancy in their lives and a genuine loneliness that they try to dispel but cannot break out of. For them real connection has become the Impossible Dream, and the more enmeshed they are in constant diversionary activities, the less likely this connection has of becoming real.

72

In the previous chapters I have talked about ways to become reconnected with your deeper self. Here I want you to realize that you can do this, and face your own *problems* around meeting and touching men—if you still have them. I hope you won't mind if I give you still a few more suggestions for ways to strengthen that important sense of self, necessary to become the successful, seductive man.

Meditation. Many people think that meditation is a part of Eastern religious practices, and it can only be done with a "mantra," or sacred word, that is delivered to them by a guru or religious instructor. Also, that it requires years of discipline to perfect. None of that is true. Meditation has been practiced by all religions and by many nonreligious people as well. It has been scientifically proven to be an excellent grounding practice. There are many forms of meditation, but basically what it does is return you to your inner self, to that greater Self that we still try to block out every day with the endless business and busyness of living.

The easiest way to start meditating is simply by counting breaths. Sit up in a quiet place, feet resting comfortably on the floor, relaxed. Breathe deeply, but not in a forced manner, and count each complete breath, inhaling and exhaling until you reach one hundred. Pay enough attention to your breathing that other concerns and thoughts start to disappear: you don't have to fight them, they will start to go away naturally on their own.

You will find that by the time you hit one hundred, you've relaxed enough to feel restored. If you do this once a day for a week, you've begun a meditation regimen. Meditation can also work beautifully in stressful situations, and even taking five minutes to do it can work better than, say, a coffee break or a martini. Also, you can add touching into the meditative process and combine slow, meditative breathing while touching another man. This turns touching into a delicious, extended "dessert" activity, and is different from the forced, rushed kind of touching too many men engage in, in either anonymous sex or masturbation, where getting to orgasm as fast as possible becomes the goal.

Another thing to keep in mind is that if you feel you have been locked up in your brain too long, any form of physical activity can work as an excellent prologue to touching. Exercise, especially aerobic, but any form of physical movement that de-stresses you, and brings you inner peace, is good for this. If this movement involves mediation too, such as yoga or Tai Chi, all the better. Also sports (in a supportive environment where you don't feel embarrassed because you're not a professional athlete) can be sensuous and exciting. They can get you out of the aloneness that bothers you and keeps you away from other men, and they can also develop assertiveness.

And some assertiveness is good when you're dealing with seduction.

If you are asking, "What has all this got to do with me being able to seduce guys?" I hope I have answered that already. The important thing is to develop a feeling within you that you are now *complete* enough to seek out and touch someone else. Too many men feel that they are *only* complete when another person is involved; this forces them into a hard-core cruising corner of desperation and neediness that is definitely not seductive.

In short, you want to be able to feel as whole by yourself as you are with other people. Feeling and appearing centered and in touch with your own self is definitely seductive and conducive to touching other men.

I hope that these two concepts work with you.

WORK FOR YOU: Practice breathing meditation for three days. Allow yourself at least twenty minutes to do this. If you want, you can also combine slow, regular breathing with the use of a meditative word, like Om, on the exhale. Combine this breathing with the slow self-touching that we practiced in Chapter Fifteen. If you want to extend the meditative period to a longer amount of time, you can also explore more self-touching now, including touching erogenous areas such as your nipples, groin, feet, and genitals. Some men here might get into masturbation, and if this does happen, don't berate yourself for it. You are getting closer to the deeper, inner self. The idea is to forgo orgasm and not get into your usual stock of masturbatory fantasies but, again, allow yourself to explore the larger space of your breathing, your senses, and the sheer splendor of your own deeper self. There is a landscape waiting here that many men have never experienced before. It is amazingly satisfying, so don't get locked into masturbatory images of hot men you can't have because in reality they are not present.

You're here, and that is what counts.

19 Advanced Touching: Do's and Don'ts

CHAPTER

"All men need to be touched. There is no place in America that suffers more from the legacy of rugged individualism than the male body. As boys enter their teen years, they are overtly and covertly initiated into the loneliness and isolation of being a man."

Joseph Kramer, founder of Body Electric

If you feel that things are working in both your favors—he is right for you, and he's making some indications that you are right for him—now you can get somewhat more physical. This means that you might have moved out of the original setting you were in (such as a bar, club, party, etc.) or found an area of this setting that you felt was more conducive to privacy, or perhaps you have simply established more of a sense of privacy between the two of you. But you can now start touching his face more, getting physically closer to him, leaning in slightly more toward him.

You are now perhaps chest to chest, with this wonderful delicious sense that even clothed you are sharing some of the same space. In fact, your breathing may start to become a bit more rushed from excitement.

That's wonderful. That's part of the lovely anticipation of what's going on, what can happen, and what seems ready to happen.

This does not mean automatically that you are going to hit the sack—that may not happen for a week (or a year!). But it does mean that his very presence near you has real satisfactions of its own. And there is the fact that you've brought him to a point where he's comfortable with you—you've established some trust; and you've brought out your own delight in just being close to him, which he can feel. So you're at that point where the erotic imagination starts to flick its little switches, like mini-lights going on in various parts of your mind and body. There may be actual autonomic responses happening; you might start to sweat more, breathe a little harder, or even blush.

The blushing part is beautiful. I love blushing, experiencing that fresh sense of delight, wonder, and amazement with someone. However, some men are embarrassed by this. They feel that this is a signal that they are green, inexperienced, not cool enough, and (sadly enough, for them) a loser.

Nothing can be further from the truth, and if you find him blushing, stammering, and showing shyness in your presence, then be extremely pleased. It means, in truth, that he finds you so marvelous that he can barely contain his feelings and pleasure.

Compliment him on the fact that he still can be delighted; he's not so completely jaded that no new meeting leaves him unmoved and untouched. You can begin by remarking something like, "It's all right. I'm not sure what to say either."

Or, "It's nice just to have this quiet moment with you."

In other words: neither of you has to have the right lines now. This is about reaction, and feeling good. It's not about being the world's coolest person, or coming up with TV sitcom rejoinders.

The thrill of seduction is that you really don't know what's going to happen. And just as no artist knows exactly how the painting is going to turn out, but leaves room for play in it, allow both of you room for some unexpected responses.

Especially, if you choose now to kiss him.

That first kiss can be so marvelous that it should be bottled and turned into one of those zillion-dollar-an-ounce fragrances. I say "can be" because sometimes it's not. Again, we have the touch-phobic culture working. If you do feel that things are working well enough to zoom in for a close-up, it's better to start off extremely light—as in, a very simple brush of your lips on his cheeks.

People have this idea that kissing must be an all-out, full-tilt, deep-throat affair. That has destroyed huge fields of wonderful potential kisses, all those opportunities for kissing you've missed out on because you were sure that it had to be either a hundred-and-fifty-percent or nothing at all.

In truth, a very soft tender kiss on the cheek can make many men cream in their pants. Suddenly time stops. In the Middle Ages these kisses were called "brother kisses," and those knights knew what they were talking about. There is something so infinitely beautiful about it, especially when you do it at the right time, that it almost makes the rest of the kissing show seem anticlimactic. Leaning in and kissing him on his cheek also means that you are now setting things up in a way that allows both of your wishes to happen in a nonthreatening environment.

This means:

He can now kiss you back, if he wants to.

Or, you can pull back and see what is happening with him. Is he shocked, delighted, smiling, puzzled, or all of the above?

If you are in a comfortable (and appropriate enough) situation, you can, once you've pulled back and seen that he is responding nicely, "go back in," that is, get closer to him again. And by keeping at least one hand lightly on him, you can make it evident that you'd like to kiss him once more.

> "Next thing I knew, I was down there with her,
> and we were staring into each other's eyes, and
> locked in each other's arms, and straining to get
> closer."
> James M. Cain, *The Postman Always Rings Twice*

There are, though, things you should *not* do at this point, and unfortunately a lot of men do them.

Things Not to Do.

1) Don't lunge in with the whole tongue. As the Valley Girls used to say, "Gag me with a spoon!" So many guys don't understand this. You don't go from a simple cheek kiss to full tongue. It's rude, tacky, and juvenile.

2) Don't grope him. This is the worst seduction *faux pas*. You're not here to check out his equipment, see if his pecs are real, his butt's tight, and kick the tires. Doing this sets a man on edge, makes him feel defensive, and marks you as an aggressive jerk to avoid.

3) Don't try to undress him, especially if you're still in a public space. Don't try to rearrange his clothes, loosen his tie, mess up his hair, or pull off his sweater and jacket. I don't know why guys are dumb enough to do this, but they do.

4) Don't leave tooth marks. You're *not* Dracula.

5) Don't tickle him, goose him, or make him feel that he has no idea what you're going to do next—and he doesn't want to find out.

6) Finally— you'd think this goes without saying—don't pull out a bottle of poppers (amyl nitrate), drugs, your own bottle of whatever, or try to get him drunk, drugged, or disoriented.

Any of these things can make a man feel that he is no longer in control of his space, and he needs to get out of there as fast as possible.

So, now might be a good time to start some conversation again, to make him aware that you are deeply appreciative of him, and enjoying the hell out of yourself as well.

"I'm really glad I met you."

"I don't usually feel so comfortable with someone."

"Are you all right?"

This last question is *always* good. So few people demonstrate any interest in anyone else (unless they're prospective clients or customers), that simply asking "Are you all right?" can be a beautiful gesture. He may also feel that now is the time to start kissing you more. You're inviting it, and this is something he may want to do himself.

So now may be a good time for me to talk about kissing in more advanced terms.

WORK FOR YOU: Bring back a memory of the first kiss you ever had—that is, real kiss, we're not talking about Mommy or Aunt Glenda. How did it feel? Did you feel lighter than air for a moment, like you were ready to float up to the ceiling? Did you ever have a playful, teasing kiss that made you want to dive in for more? Did you ever kiss someone who was so good at it that you felt lost for a second? Think of these kisses and how wonderful it would be to have them again, in a seductive situation that you are in control of.

CHAPTER 20

Kissing: Advanced Lessons

"You must remember this, / A kiss is still a kiss /
A sigh is just a sigh."
Herman Hupfeld, "As Times Goes By"

A lot of men have terrible problems with kissing; then there are men who were just born doing it. They are great kissers. You've probably met a few of them. Kissing them is entering into this intoxicating world. You feel slightly drunk, dizzy, and delighted when you stop. In fact, you don't want to stop. I don't know if the movies invented kissing, at least the kind of kissing that Americans are famous for, but who can forget some of the screen's great kisses, like Montgomery Cliff and Elizabeth Taylor's close-up kiss in *A Place in the Sun*, and of course Burt Lancaster and Deborah Kerr's rolling-on-the-beach kiss in *From Here to Eternity*?

Both kisses have something in common: You are not just kissing with your mouth, but with your whole body.

I remember the first time a man kissed me, I mean *really* kissed me. It wasn't a great kiss. In fact, it was pretty awful! He was more interested in overwhelming me than in making me feel connected with him. Connected wasn't even in the picture as he planted a big one on me.

And his breath smelled awful; not fresh, not appealing, and not good!

But, once initiated into the magic land of kisses, I wasn't going to stop. And one of my friends at college at the University of Georgia, back in the Jurassic mid-1960s, was one of the world's great kissers. As in: Wow! Like, earth-shaking. I had a huge crush on him, and during several late-night, hard-drinking sessions we ended up making out. I used some of his techniques with girls, and soon got the rep of being . . . well, a great kisser!

What is it that makes a great kisser?

First let's put to bed an old myth: the fact that you don't have chiseled, perfect, cute-as-a-rosebud lips does not mean you're not going to be a good kisser. I've known guys with thin, anemic, scrawny little lips who are tornado-level kissers. I've also known gorgeous guys who look like magazine models who could not kiss worth a damn. Mostly because they were not interested in someone else enough to do it right. Some things can be a total turn-off in the kissing department.

First, of course, is your breath. This is for the most part one of the easiest things to deal with, and we are living in an age of high TV consumer advertising when having bad breath is verboten, even in dogs. Even Fido can't have bad breath anymore. So why do some men still persist in having bad breath, and then want to kiss you?

So, starting with this foundation, check your breath. That is fairly easy to do with the old hand-blowing method. Bring your palm up to your mouth, so that the heel of it is at your chin. Angle it slightly away from your mouth, and blow on it. If your breath smells objectionable, something's wrong.

However, if you've had a breath problem for a long time, you are so used to the way it smells that no matter how many times you do this, it will still smell "normal" to you.

Hammacher Schlemmer now offers an electronic breath checker. It checks the level of acids and alkali in your breath, and reads it out as a number. But, I think a better idea is to start practicing real oral hygiene. This means flossing every day with something like Oral-B's Ultra Floss, which adds a fine fuzz to the length of the floss, like running a little brush between your teeth, down to your gum line. Brushing your teeth between meals, and use a mouthwash. Also very important, use a tongue scraper or tongue brush. You can find these in most drugstores. The tongue is one of the main culprits in objectionable breath. There are also mouthwashes specifically designed for your breath, that maintain the proper acid balance in your mouth.

Other things can affect your breath besides eating a garlic and onion sandwich. Sinus drainage can get down into your mouth and stay there; using a sinus decongestant can be helpful if you're having sinus or allergy problems. Also, a condition known as dry mouth, which means that you don't produce enough saliva to naturally wash out some of the germs and bacteria that find a resting place in your mouth. People who have dry mouth can gargle twelve times a day and still have bad breath. The answer again is a good drugstore, where saliva substitutes can be found.

Once you start doing these things, you'll find your trips to the dentist a lot nicer, but don't skip them. Having your teeth cleaned regularly is a key to good oral health, and good kissing. This helps prevent tooth decay, and tooth decay tastes horrible. I mean *awful*. If you're not aware that your teeth are decaying, because you're used to it and staying away from the dentist, then you're in really bad shape.

Robert Burns was famous for his little couplet: "Oh what gifts the good gods gee us / to see ourselves as others see us?" "Gee" was Scottish dialect for "give." But an even better gift would be to smell ourselves as others smell us!

Also helpful, Listerine now makes a very convenient "travel" form of mouthwash, in really cool flavors like mint and cinnamon, little dissolvable sheets that you can use anyplace. They quickly disappear in your mouth, and leave you with a quick whiff of freshness.

Don't rely on breath mints instead of real oral care. Breath mints can help if you're a smoker, but at some point they will stop working and you're left again with the same old dragon breath.

This does not mean that you have to brush, floss, gargle, and mint every moment of the day. There are moments when smelling something on a man's breath can be wonderful, as long as it does not overwhelm you and there is a basic foundation of freshness there.

Now that we've got that out of the way, on to the kiss.

As Lauren Bacall said to Humphrey Bogart, "You know how to whistle, just pucker up and blow!" Kissing does require some of that puckering, but what makes a good kisser is that the lips are relaxed, even while slightly puckered. If you are a stone-stiff puckerer, try practicing relaxing your lips. Also, approaching him, getting your lips to touch his, then opening the lips slightly adds a measure of beautiful intimacy to a kiss. You can practice this by slowly repeating the word "please," over and over. The "P-l-e" sound creates a natural pucker and release.

Also, draw closer. Feel like you're melting into him, like your body and his are becoming as close to one as you can get. Not suffocating him, but just this sense of real, almost magnetic closeness.

Once you invite this closeness, it is difficult for anyone to resist it—especially when, inside, most men don't want to. What you want to establish is that you're not trying to direct him, overpower him, or coerce him into doing what you want; you are simply creating an environment of wonderful, powerful closeness. This wonder and power come from the two of you together, not any single one of you.

While you're doing this, let your hand brush tenderly across his face or neck, and don't try to squeeze him with your other hand. Just try to make him feel comfortable, even protected by you. I've known men who were so unused to this sense of comfort and protection who, in the past, had felt so exposed by their own sexual desires, dreading fears of rejection, ridicule, and hurt, that they began to cry once they relaxed. Strings of feelings were coming out of them, and they could not separate them.

If anything like that happens, just be happy that you've been able to make him feel so at ease with himself, and with you.

Then there is necking.

Necking is a wonderfully old-fashioned term for nuzzling, kissing, and fondling other places besides the lips. These include the ears, the chin, the throat, and, depending upon levels of undress, the shoulders, elbows (a tremendously sensitive area), inner arms, wrists, palms, and fingers. I adore ears, and love the places behind them, the rims of them, the immediate inner ear, and the lobe. Earrings and ear studs makes these areas even more delightful, but you have to be careful not to put stress on pierced areas. (This warning goes double for pierced nipples, but I'll go into that later.)

Kissing and necking are two pillars of seductive behavior, but there are many other activities that you should be conscious of (and try!). The next chapter goes into them and if for some reason you have not been using them in the past, now is the time to learn about them.

WORK FOR YOU: Do the breath assessment I wrote about earlier in this chapter. Assign a time every day for flossing, brushing, and gargling. One of life's most miserable disappointments is meeting a handsome guy with bad breath. And one of life's joys is finding a guy who rewards you with breath so nice that all you want to do is get closer to him.

Also, practice using your lips in new ways: lifting the corners a bit with a slight smirk, puckering up slightly, then running your tongue gently over them. One of the most seductive men I've ever met had a habit, when he was interested in you, of moistening the center of his top lip and keeping his tongue there for a few seconds. At that point, all you wanted to do was kiss him.

CHAPTER 21

Nine Very Seductive Activities You Should Try

These activities, or "colors," should be on every seductive man's palette. You might have a few of your own, so don't limit yourself to these. You'll also notice that these are not full-fledged sexual activities, but they can lead naturally to sex, and they're fun in themselves. I have not put them in any order of use or importance; you should let the occasion decide how you want to use them.

1) Nuzzling: getting very close with your face, especially with light pressure from your cheeks, nose, brow, and mouth. Part of nuzzling is using your slightly opened lips as a paintbrush, softly stroking his neck, cheeks, the bridge and ridge of his nose (very sensitive places), his eyelids, and brow. You can also do this on his lips (nuzzling on and with the lips is never a bad thing), but don't forget his neck, shoulders, chest, stomach, and other parts. Horses are famous nuzzlers and do it simply as a sign of affection. So take a tip from any smart horse: Nuzzle, but don't nag.

2) Nibbling: taking soft, small, toothless love "snacks" all over him, like little fishes sucking in water. Nibbling is part kissing, part sucking, all delight. It also works beautifully on nipples, navels, inner thighs, and other more private areas, once you get down to that.

3) Tasting: exerting very small amounts of pressure *with* the teeth. This is not to be confused with actual bites, although some men do get into very low pressure "love biting," which can be extremely exciting. What I am against is leaving marks: a very good way to scare him off, if he cannot explain that hickey at work the next day. However, the right degree and technique with tasting can drive him up a wall and keep him there.

4) Cupping: using your hands as a "cup," fingers together, palms softly moving, either to bring him closer to you or to run your hands over the terrain of his face and body. Cupping is also beautiful on buttocks, scrotums, and other areas that fit nicely in the palm(s) of your hand(s).

5) Stroking: fingers apart, applying the smallest, nicest amount of pressure as you explore him tactilely. We now think of stroking as being synonymous with masturbating, which leaves a lot of the stroking repertory behind. What you want to do is liberate your fingers, so that each one gets to explore him separately as well as together. You can also use the sides of your hands, as well as the backs of them to stroke.

A good way to practice stroking (besides the best way, by just stroking someone else) is to run your fingers over something very pleasantly tactile, like velvet or suede, and then see how many variations you can come up with on the simple basic technique of simply pushing your palms and fingers tips through it.

6) Tweaking: very small pinches, done to bring nerve endings to a higher level of sensitivity and excitement. Tweaking should never be painful, but just teasing enough to make him want you not to stop until you do something that's even better. Nipples respond beautifully to tweaking. But the back of the neck, the bridge of the nose, the biceps, and the back of the upper leg, just below the butt, tweak nicely, as well as any part of the buttocks themselves.

7) Licking. To be done with the whole tongue, or just the tip of it. Licking is a universally nice activity, but some overlooked and underserviced places to really explore licking are the ears (the backs and lobes of which can be very sensitive), the crook of the elbow, the underarm area especially the skin leading from the underarm to the nipple, the entire palm and the fingers, the hollow of the throat, and the temples. Most men feel they know everything about licking, then go only to the most obvious places, like the navel or groin. Don't just use your tongue like a snake, darting in and out; use it like a steady eye reading the inner nerves of his soul.

8) Pulsing and pulse-kissing. Touching a pulse point lightly and feeling the pressure of his heart beating and directing the blood as it approaches the surface of his body is very intimate, as is placing your own pulse points on him. In ancient times men joined or linked pulse points to show brotherly affection, trust, and deeper nonverbal communication. There are numerous pulse points on the body. These are meridians used in acupressure, and they are very sensitive to any form of attention or touch. Your own pulse points are sensitive as well. Slowly running the pulse point at the first joint of your index finger over a man's face and anatomy is extremely sexy, as is kissing, nib-

bling, or nuzzling the pulse points of his wrists, neck, temples, groin, or ankles.

9) Restriction and exertion. Using some of the force of your muscles on him, allow him to exert against you at moments, so that he can feel the life force of your body against his, and return his own power to you. Some men may find this a prelude to S & M activities, or erotic wrestling, which under the right circumstances can be wonderful. (The wrong circumstances is that he had no idea this was coming or what will happen next—so don't make him feel threatened by this. Use only enough power to make him feel excited.)

WORK FOR YOU: Think of an erotic situation you haven't had that would turn you on to the hilt, now think about how you can introduce this to another man. As the valorous seducer, you should put yourself enough in control to ask for what you want, or try to indicate it. Many men are too repressed to ask for what they want sexually, except in a porno chatroom setting where it becomes simply more masturbatory material. But asking for sexual favors is extremely revealing, and bonds the two of you with a deeper intimacy.

Now, make a list of things, erotic and otherwise, that you'd like either to do, or to have done to you. Making this list can be liberating in itself. If you feel that even writing in this book is too "public" for such things, then make your list on a separate piece of paper.

WORK SPACE
Your very special list!—

_____

_____

_____

_____

_____

_____

_____

22 Knowing When to Stop

"But fine though they may be, bachelors' dinners, like bachelors' lives, can not endure forever. The time came for breaking up. One by one, the bachelors took their hats, and two by two, and arm-in-arm they descended ..."
Herman Melville, *The Paradise for Bachelors*

After you get into the kissing phase of the seduction (that is, if you have gone that far), the next thing is knowing when to stop. Some men will ask, "Why stop, I'm having such a good time?"

Because knowing when to stop, just like knowing when to initiate your seductive behavior, is very important. You don't want to overwhelm the intimate boundaries of the situation. In my book *How to Survive Your Own Gay Life* I said, in no uncertain terms: "Intimacy is *finite.*" Your love may go on forever, but your ability to be intimate does not.

You need to come up for air. He does too. In fact, he may be dying for it. You don't want to make him feel pressured, suffocated, or pushed into something he's not ready for. Also, you want to show that you can invite this intimacy, but there is more to come later. So, after a comfortable, enticing first course of kissing, whether you are in a more-or-less public or a very private place, move away from him, slightly.

But maintain some physical contact with him.

You can do that simply by keeping one hand lightly on him. Don't grip him, but keep contact, as if you're dancing slowly with him. Show him that you are not rejecting him (in other words, there's no one better in the area), you're just allowing him some air and space, and you need it, too. Now is the time to say, "I really enjoyed that." Or:

"It was wonderful kissing you."

"That was very nice."

"I really wanted to do that. I hope you liked it, too."

At this point, you don't have to come up with a line of scintillating conversation, which is one of the nice things about physical interactions: You no longer have to impress him with your command of polished TV dialogue.

What I mean by that is that we are now so used to clever, pre-plotted ("Cool!") interactions and dialogues that real spontaneity, with all the "Uhh"s, "Duh"s, and "Whachamean?"s thrown in, disappoints us. So many guys feel socially and sexually castrated as soon as talk stops, or comes to a comfortable lull. This is also a symptom of having too many phone relationships. (Actually, phone time has now become fairly intimate—too many people only keep up brief Twitter connections with their friends.) When the talk stops, everything else is supposed to, also, and some men start to feel really bashful and socially inept at this point.

What's important is the connection between your eyes, hands, and lips and his. Since you've already established enough of this connection to work with, you can leave the one-liners and zingers at home. One of the great benefits of understanding seduction is that don't have to have Jerry Seinfeld and Larry David writing dialogue for you anymore.

You just have to understand the uses of dialogue. And its main use is simply to bring him closer to you.

The other good part about knowing when to stop, is that it leaves him wanting more. Now is not the time to be so "in his face" that he can't wait to get rid of you. A lot of men become so scared that it will be "Outsville" as soon as they stop that initial kissing that they turn the magic of it into a dragged-out ordeal, like a movie that starts out wonderful and just does not know where to end. By editing the action, you leave space to begin negotiations for what will come next.

WORK FOR YOU: Identify three situations, sexual or social, where things went on too long. You were bored, couldn't wait to leave. See these as three situations that needed "editing," that is, someone deciding that now was the time to stop.

WORK SPACE:

_____

_____

_____

_____

_____

_____

_____

_____

_____

_____

23 Coming Up with the Right Proposition

"Isn't it rich? / Are we a pair? / Me here at last on the ground / You in mid-air."
Stephen Sondheim,
"Send in the Clowns" from *A Little Night Music*

Now that you've stopped, it will probably be up to you to decide where to take this next. As the seducer, you should not have to count on him to do this, even if it's in his mind, too. After all, you are the one dealing the cards, so why not be the one to decide when and how you'll at least bring up the "closing"?

A bit of sage advice: Knowing when and how to close is what creates what that beloved father-figure Donald Trump calls "the Deal." And we do live in an Age of Deals. Once, Romeo might have jumped up to Juliet's balcony, and from then on there was no question of what was going to happen, just how to get away with it. Now, Romeo would have to say, "OK, Juliet, we've carried this conversation so far. I'm not sure about this—we've got your overworked schedule and mine to figure out. Have you got your Blackberry handy? I think that on the—"

Of course, that is all predicated on whether Romeo, to begin with, saw any future in his "thing" with Juliet. So, here again, a little mastery of details helps.

First, impress on him what you'd like.

"I'd like to see you again. Are you busy later?"

"I'd like to invite you over to my place."

"I'd like to get to know you better. Can I get your phone number?"

"I'd like to give you my phone number and e-mail address."

What you're doing here is not hitting the ball awkwardly into his court. You're not making him respond, and then having him worry if he's doing the right thing. Don't say:

"Would you like to see me again?"

"Do you think we can see each other again?"

"How would you feel about going home with me?"

These questions put him into a situation where he has to make the decision, and for some men that alone is problematic. They will kill dragons for you, they will do *anything* you ask. But don't expect them to decide to do it.

What you want to do is make sure he doesn't feel manipulated, pressured, or pushed.

He may be directed, skillfully, toward the same direction you wanted to go, but—hey!—that's a genuine part of seduction, too. The important thing is that he doesn't feel pushed into it.

Here I'll go through two very normal, almost expected scenarios, and you can see what your own reaction would be. We'll call you *You* and call him (what else?) *Him*.

Scenario One

You: "This has been nice. I've really liked being with you. I'd like to spend more time with you. How does that sound?"

Note: Don't say, "What do you think about that?"

Him: "Well, I'm not sure."

You: "I'd really like that, if it's possible."

Him: "I don't know. I mean, I didn't expect to do that."

You: "I didn't expect to, either. But like I said, I really like being with you."

Him: "No, I don't think I can do that."

You: "That's all right. I'd like to see you again at some point. I'd like to give you my phone number."

Him: "I'm not sure I should take it."

So, what do you do now? He is giving you some resistance. This may not happen, but suppose it does? The answer is simple. You revert back to what you want. This does not mean that you're saying, "It's okay to change your mind." "Decide later." "Don't worry." You are simply saying:

You: "I'd like it if you would."

Scenario Two

You: "I can't believe how nice it's been being with you. It's made me really happy. I'd like to see you again."

Him:"You would?"

You: "Yes, I'd like that very much."

Him: "Why?"

Now, don't go into a "smart" answer like, "Why do you think?" Don't try to put him on edge, and lob the ball back at him.

You: "Because I would. You're attractive and nice to be with."

Him: "Do you really think that?"

You: "Yes, I do. I'd like to invite you home with me."

Him: "You would? Why? You hardly know me. I'm not used to pick-ups like this."

You: "I'd like to get to know you better. Just the two of us. But I'd like to see you later if you're not ready for something else tonight. I'd like to give you my phone number."

Here you can include a complimentary question/situation: "If that's all right with you?" This is basically saying, "I'm including you in the equation, but you don't have to make the decision." So, let's repeat this with:

You: "I'd like to get to know you better. Just the two of us. But I'd like to see you later if you're not ready for something else tonight. I'd like to give you my phone number, if that's all right with you."

Note: Don't make "if that's all right with you" sound like a question as much as a statement.

Him: "Sure."

You: "Good, I'd really like it if you called me. I'll look forward to it. When can I expect a call?"

Here you're not saying "When do you think you will?" but, "When will you be making me—and you—happy, by calling me?"

Him: "I don't know. I have to think about it. I'm not sure. I'll have to, uh, lemme see, I'm not—"

You: "I'd really like it if you'd call me next week. How does that sound to you?"

The "How does that sound to you?" puts him back into the question, but does not put the weight of the question on him.

Dealing with the "FDG" Response

Sometimes in extreme circumstances, you will get what I call the "FDG" response. "FDG" stands for: "Fuck You! Drop Dead! Go to Hell!"

In other words, you've really barked up the wrong tree.

This can happen. Some people are simply not put together in a manner that allows them to respond to you in a humane and open way. The idea that you are opening up a situation that can have some indecision in it means that they have to snap it closed, even if later they regret doing it. They've been programmed to respond that way. They have been convinced that this *is* the appropriate, hostile, snappy, offensive way to deal with you, because you, after all, have made the utterly revolting suggestion that *they* are worth your time. If this happens, and you feel that you are getting nowhere—in fact, you are being abused—then make him feel that you are the one initiating this, and you, not he, are the one in control.

Him: "Go home with you? Are you crazy? I don't want to see you at all. I don't want your phone number. I don't want anything! This is ridiculous!"

You: "I'm sorry that you feel that way. I wish you didn't. But I can certainly respect your feelings. It's not easy for a lot of guys to meet someone. No matter what, they're not up to it. I can understand that."

You can see here that you've placed the emphasis upon yourself. *You* feel sorry, *you* wish things were different; you're giving him respect and you're understanding him.

Stand your ground. Don't run away, although rejection does hurt (and it is why I've introduced the importance of valor early on). By standing your ground, you will make most men realize how childish they're behaving. He may even go through a change right there. Or he may do it later, at which point he may come over to you. What you need to show him is that you are in control, and his own childish behavior does not affect you radically—you can see it and feel it—but it does not destroy you or make you run away.

You don't want to attack him. But you might want to back off a bit physically. This means removing eye contact from him for a moment, and then coming back with your own feelings intact.

He Has Accepted Your Information

OK, things have worked out. And he has accepted your telephone number, e-mail address, etc. Now it's time for you to step forward and ask: "Is there some way I can reach you?"

The response to this should be: "Sure, let me give you my number."

But what if it's: "I don't know. I don't usually give out my number."

Again, revert to what you want:

"I'd really like to have some way of reaching you. I'd like your e-mail address."

You may suspect that you are going through a lot of effort for a feeling that is unrequited. He doesn't give a damn, and you do. But don't let that immediate cold shower feeling deter you. And keep the following concepts in mind:

You are the one initiating the action. Instead of staying there on the sidelines, wondering why nothing is happening, which is what too many guys do. So, like a star performer, you are now "center" on the stage of life, causing things to happen. And this is always impressive.

Also, don't expect your feelings to be mirrored *exactly* by him. They may come out in a very different way, but reach the same destination. He really *does* want to see you; he'd really *love* to hop in the sack with you; he's probably much more *crazy* about you than he can possibly let on—but the sad, crazy, surprising thing is that at that moment he probably doesn't even know it. So, your own positiveness, your valorous actions, have opened up for him some possibilities that include both of you, whether he can see them at the moment or not.

WORK FOR YOU: Read over the scenarios I have given you in this chapter. Get to know them and the concepts behind them. In many ways, these scenarios are based on older forms of manners: of extending yourself to another person, holding your own ground while conceding some space to another, sending out a message but in a kind and constructive way. The more familiarity you have with these ideas, the easier it will be to make dates and "close the deal," and the less alone and unprepared you will feel. What is important is that you feel in control of yourself and the space you are creating between the two of you. After all, you valorously initiated this, so the terms should be basically yours.

CHAPTER 24

Alien" Monster Raises Its Ugly Head: Dealing with Rejection

"You cannot be deterred by things that are other people's problems."
Leontyne Price, Metropolitan Opera diva

We live now in what I call the "culture of rejection." It is all around us as part of our consumerist society, where everything, and I mean EVERYTHING, is shown and offered to you, but little is actually given. It's a constant striptease, on a very demeaning, ugly level. Part of the rejection aspect is that in our media-controlled, info-flooded world there is too much to deal with. You are given a gazillion choices, but there is still nothing to wear; there are sixty channels on TV, and still nothing to watch, because most of it is just a variation on the same theme of yet more choices to . . . reject.

Reject becomes the only protection, and often the only immediately available response. The choices do not add more excitement, curiosity, and pleasure to your life. They do not bring you any closer to a feeling of satisfaction with yourself. They only clog up the route to that satisfaction.

Romantic life has certainly mirrored this phenomenon. Now there are more and more reasons to reject a guy, instead of the simple, self-affirming curiosity that makes you want to get to know him more, and on an intimate level. You're *too* busy, *too* stressed, *too* fried; and he doesn't look exactly how you wanted or isn't cool enough, bright enough, or good enough to be what you're sure he should be.

Reject.

We now have super-busy, DSL-speed, fast-forward dating, micro-dating, and audition dating, where guys (and girls, too) confront one another for five minutes to see if they're suitable partners. There is no real human backstory and little attempt at seeing someone as more than an irritating commercial for himself.

With the Internet, phone sex, ad dating, and about half a dozen forms of matchmaking *yentahood* out there (for a price), you're in this wilderness of available prospects, choices, and prospective suitors who are all lined up there, with ninety-nine out of a hundred possibilities ending up:

Reject.

As a result, rejection is now a huge fear because so many of us have been rejected so often. We have to be. After all, rejection goes both ways, even though I'd guess that if you're reading this, you're sure it hits you more than you hit it. This is not to say that in the past people did not get rejected, but they did not have to work so hard to find ways and reasons to do it. Also, there was more social fabric and adhesion around to allow meetings and possibilities to happen (although much of that statement may just be nostalgic fantasies; face it, the "good old days" are only good because they're gone).

Still, you have the question of how to deal with rejection and not be hurt and deterred by it.

Remember:

Most of the time, men are not rejecting *you*. They're rejecting a situation they feel they can't control, and the fact that you are bringing more stress (and lack of control) into either a socially or sexually-charged situation. For many men, these situations are no longer pleasant—and they have no idea how to make them so. What they are really interested in is a way out of their own loneliness, and, to be frank, horniness; let's not discount that as being below us, it ain't. Strangely enough, many of these outlets from loneliness don't seem to be working. As I have said before, meeting other people is natural to humans, and men want social and sexual satisfaction. You'd think, therefore, they'd open themselves up to a lot more invitations, propositions, and encounters.

They don't.

What they are saying is that they are not up to an interaction with *you* because they've been programmed not to have it. They lack the social training, skills, and security to be interested in you. Although meeting people is a natural human desire, before that desire can be satisfied, there needs to be some feeling of personal security and safety allowing the desire to work. And you need to feel that your desire is welcomed and will be honored.

In our competitive and insecure world, this is often not the case. We've ended up with a lot of overstressed, lonely people who automatically push the "reject" button because that is the only way they can operate and feel they can control things.

They don't feel safe and secure enough not to push it.

Now, some of this feeling may be real—we've experienced the AIDS pandemic; the emergence of even newer STDs; 9-11; the emergence of the Christian Right and its imposition of "family values" (I now meet dozens of gay Christians who are embarrassed by their own gay community, the very community that allowed them to come out as gay in the first place); a corporatized world that demands people live, eat, and breathe their jobs, an extremely insecure job market; and the specter of the bottom dropping out of the financial environment that keeps most of us afloat.

So a lot of our fears are real, and so is the rejection that comes with them. Where does that leave you?

First, understand that being rejected is often not a statement about you as much as it is about him. No matter how wonderful or complete *you* are, you just can't come up to his fantasy "ideal," whatever that is. This ideal is often referred to as his "type," or his "preferred match," or however he may put it, but it is still very much a fantasy. You may see him as someone you can be attracted to, approach, and show interest in. He's seeing you as . . . well, it's hard to say. The fact is, you don't know how he's seeing you or what has brought him to see you that way. His rejection means that at the moment he can't see you as the person you really are, and he is letting you know this in spades.

Sometimes that's actually good. Even a stone rejection is better than a coy phoniness that's only wasting your time. The important thing is, no matter who (or what) rejects you, you are not going to reject yourself. You know your own value, and how hard it has been to get to the point where you understand it.

No matter who you are (and what your assets, talents, looks, and advantages may be), it's not up to you—or even possible for you—to fulfill every one of his expectations and demands. You can work at some of them, but if he's foolish enough to come up with all of his demands at once and use *them* to reject you, then what he's saying is that he's unable to see you. All he can see are his own demands, things he's sure he deserves. It is as simple at that. You can't make him grow up, but you can behave like a grownup yourself. And this is always attractive to the right person.

Some people will say I'm just calling, "Sour grapes!"

Rejection is still rejection and it's going to hurt, no matter what.

But you should never question (or *self-reject*) that part of you that is going out there with frankness, honesty, and courage, working to achieve your own goals and desires. Any rejection of you should *never* dismiss or diminish that. As you become more skillful at seduction, and are rejected less, you will be able to see that part of yourself and admire it.

And if he can't—that's sad.

But, as Scarlett O'Hara said, "Tomorrow is another day."

WORK FOR YOU: Remember a past rejection you've had. How would you view this person now? Do you still feel pained by it, or have you reached the point where you feel that this might have been an entanglement you didn't need, and shouldn't have? How do you see yourself as that person from your past? How are you changing?

Make a list of three guys who you feel rejected you. You may not even know their names (a bar cold-shoulder; a quick look on the street that was not returned). Try to see the full circumstances of the rejection. You were not in control then. Now let go of these rejections, and as many rejections as you can that hold you back.

WORK SPACE:
Your list (three guys)—

_____

_____

_____

_____

_____

_____

_____

_____

_____

_____

25 Jack Climbs the Beanstalk and Finds— You Reject *Him*

"He had noticed, further, that Tadzio's teeth were imperfect, rather jagged and bluish, without a healthy glaze, and of that peculiar brittle transparency which the teeth of chorotic people often show."

Thomas Mann, *Death in Venice*

On the other hand, at some point you may find yourself rejecting him. There are lots of reasons why this happens, and I'm sure you can find several yourself. Sometimes it just did not work. He turned out to be more effort than you wanted to go through, or there was a casualness in the relationship that could not be masqueraded as anything else. He was not Mr. Right, but was definitely Mr. Right Away. Mr. Right Away should be a fairly glorious role in anybody's life; you were really happy when he came along, and now you've decided that things have "run their natural course."

This can happen at any time during your "seduction" of him. It can happen twenty minutes after you've walked over to him, twenty hours, twenty days. The possibility of your rejecting him is just as much a part of the equation as his rejecting you.

But before you reject anyone, keep these ideas in mind:

Are you rejecting him because he's *really* interested in you and that bothers you? Are you thinking, What's his problem? Is he so desperate that he wants (of all people) *me*? I know this sounds like Groucho Marx's famous remark about never wanting join any club that would have him as a member, but often we have a feeling that if a man is too "easy," there must be something wrong with him. We cannot take seriously the idea that some events and the people involved with them fall naturally into place. He's not crazy about you because he really *is* crazy and too "easy"; it's because he knows what he wants.

Be grateful that, in this case, he's smarter than you are.

On the other hand, there are guys who, for whatever reason, can't stand any form of attention unless they initiate it. Often they are too rigid to flirt, and too cold to respond. Several years ago I met a very serious young journalist at a gay science fiction convention and was taken with him, but not any more than I was with about half a dozen other guys. He built up in his mind this fantasy that I was really chasing after him, and finally accused me of it.

I smiled. "No," I assured him. "I wasn't any more 'after you' than I was 'after' anybody else."

He looked at me like he'd been slapped. The idea that I wasn't *really* "cruising" him was upsetting, offsetting any real friendliness I'd shown him. The culture of rejection was hard at work. What's important is that you nip things in the bud, even before there is a bud.

"At your age," I told him, "I was used to people paying attention to me, so I do that naturally. I'm sorry if you took it the wrong way."

I realized that he did take it the wrong way, and it undermined and threatened the rigidity of his own way of behaving.

Are you rejecting someone because you're scared that you cannot come up to his expectations?

I did this often when I was younger, because I was intimidated by men whom I felt had more money, power, or attractiveness than I had. Older men often do this with younger men; they're sure that since society stupidly devalues them, every younger man will as well. It's not true. You don't know what other men want, and how they see you. Sometimes it's hard to look at the world with the freshness of a younger man's eyes, without fear. But if you can admit to yourself how difficult it is, then you may be able to see how he's delighted by things that you do not easily see in yourself.

Unfortunately, even being older does not make you that much smarter.

Let's say you've decided that he *is* a loser, doesn't come up to everything on the bill. The choppy waters out there still have a lot more fascinating fish in the sea, and it's time to throw him overboard and stick your line out again. Sometimes you do this in a state of anger, sometimes in a state of cool reflection, but you've decided that *now* is definitely the time.

But wait. Are you *sure* that he *cannot* come up to your expectations?

Put him on hold for a while—but nicely. You "have to visit your mom in Ottawa," for instance, for a week. Give yourself a little more rope before hanging up on this relationship.

Then, after a short hiatus, come back and see what he does have to offer. You may see that all those stale jokes he tells may seem a lot funnier with some fresh air around them. Even better, he really wants to tell them to *you*. And no one else.

One of the interesting things about rejection is that the men you reject, either out of non-interest or just the dumb-ass, unintentional things any of us can do (and then stick to out of pride), come back to haunt us more than those who reject us. At some point in your life you may "get even" with a guy who rejected you (you totally snub him at a party; he sees you with a perfect "10" guy and you know *he* knows it). But the men you reject remain mysteries. Suppose you hadn't? What about those vestigial feelings, the "What-might-have-been-if-I-hadn't" questions?

So, before you show him the door forever, think about that.

WORK FOR YOU: Have you ever rejected anyone? If you did, how did you feel afterward? How do you think he felt? Do you ever wonder about him? Would you reject him now? Have you ever thought about asking him back into your life? Are you secure enough to do this? Or do you feel that it is still not something you'd do?

WORK SPACE:

What are some of your feelings?

_____

_____

_____

_____

_____

_____

_____

_____

26 Internet and Phone Seductions

"That man has a peculiar talent when anything
striking to the imagination has to be done."
Joseph Conrad, *Nostromo.*

A lot of the previous chapters of this book have dealt with one-on-one, in-person seduction. However, a large number of men now meet either on-line or on the phone. For many men this is a lot less stressful than actual "cold" meetings, pickups, and even "fix-ups" where their friends arrange meetings. One of the reasons why there's less stress is that, with online and phone meetings, there's a certain amount of preselection going on. You can go to sites geared to what you want and what you are: older men, younger guys, sites that appeal to certain body types and preferences (bears, older guys, big men, to name a few). I'm sure you're aware of all of this. There's also a certain amount of playacting going on, and this can be helpful for some men. It's easier for them to be a thoroughly butch top on the phone or online than they might be in the flesh; they can also be twenty years younger and fifteen pounds lighter (or vice versa).

If you want an online or a phone situation to be more than simply sex with a "handy" stranger (I know, this sounds like a variation on the old Zen riddle, "What is the sound of one hand slipping back and forth over a greased object?"), then some degree of truthfulness needs to be maintained in your routine. If you tell him on the phone that you're thirty-five when you're really fifty-five, and look it, then you can expect your meeting to go nowhere. The same goes online, even when pictures and/or cam shots are involved. You can Photoshop your picture until it looks like perfection, and get Tom Ford to direct your cam shot, but eventually the real you has to come through the door.

So, as in real physical seductions involving new meetings, here are some things to keep in mind while working through a digital or phone seduction.

Be interested in him. Ask about him. If he's not that interested in sharing really personal stuff with you, a complete stranger he's never met in the flesh, don't be offended.

Truthfulness, honesty, and candor are incredibly sexy. However, as in anything, don't smother him with it. You can be honest, but you don't have to gush and let everything out at once. If your online or phone persona is really different from what you are, and you are thinking about a "real time" meeting, start to move things toward reality and truth.

"Before we meet, there is some stuff I want to let you know about. I need to let you know that—"

If you've got a laundry list of "corrections" (you are not six-two, your eyes are not of blue, and you ain't ever going to see forty-two, again), balance it with what you really are like, i.e., your good points.

"I have a great sense of humor. I pride myself on being caring and considerate. I've kept myself in very good shape. I think you'll find me interesting, and I'm really looking forward to meeting you."

If this does not work, and he says, "No way," then at least you saved yourself some time and bother. But it may be that he's also hiding things, and this can give him a moment to get them off *his* chest.

A lot of men like to set up a first meeting in a neutral place, one that is safer, offers an easy way out if things don't work, and just gives you a chance to look each other over. A noisy bar is a bad idea, and so is a movie which either of you may end up hating. A restaurant or cafe is good. If the two of you've already seen pictures of each other, you *should* be easy for him to spot. If you haven't, then one of you should wear something recognizable, like a red shirt, or Yankees baseball hat.

The important thing is to make this as smooth and easy as possible.

However, that does not always happen. Nervous reactions at a meeting like this can be worse than at a cold meeting, where you can always go on the supposition that nothing has to happen. Once you've set up a meeting through an online or phone introduction, even from online or phone sex, you've already set up certain expectations and these can be hard to fulfill.

He may look like a doll and act like a jerk. He can be molten hot in a 900-number fantasy arena, and then come off like Hyacinth Bucket in person. Sometimes, because of runaway nerves, some guys get caught in a conversational loop where the only thing they can talk about *is* the most boring aspect of themselves: the day-to-day gossip at work, their family problems, leaky plumbing at home, etc.

At this point, as the seducer, you need to move things into control.

"I can see that you're as nervous about this as I am."

"You're much better looking than I thought you would be." (This may be a bold-faced lie, but it makes most men feel like you've offered them a Godiva chocolate laced with Ecstasy: in other words, feeling much better and more receptive to you.)

"Sometimes our problems seem much worse than they are, but I understand how trying that can be."

What you're doing is not putting him down, not cutting the conversation off, but making him feel that he can be secure enough to calm down and get out of the loop. You've heard enough about Ma and Pa's hemorrhoids, the evil office grinch who stole Christmas, and his cat's ear operation.

You can also volunteer things about yourself, if only to get the conversation off him.

"I think I should tell you some things about myself."

Now, bring the focus back to you for a moment. You can also be the one to initiate the proposition, if that is what you want. The proposition can be really simple, as in:

"I'd really like to see you with your clothes off."

"I'd like to see you in a more casual setting. For instance, your bedroom."

"This is really nice. We should get together sometime."

(As you can imagine, the last line means this has not been very nice, and the chances of us ever getting together are about as good as the chances of Paris Hilton getting cast as Mother Theresa.)

One of the things both of you need to look out for, especially you, as a person who understands seduction, is that you may not be on your best footing here, and neither is he. This is a pretty difficult casting call on its own, and if you had met cold and simply got to know each other without any expectations, you might really have liked one another.

Therefore, before you hit the reject button, or invite him to, keep that in mind.

Once you do take this to a *less* "neutral" setting—that is, out of the restaurant or cafe and into your or his home and (hopefully) bedroom— you will need to deal with some of the ideas I'll go into in the rest of this book. These include: Making the first move. Not making him feel cornered. Negotiating how fast to initiate sex. And, making him feel comfortable, and *sexual*, on his or your turf.

For many men, these are no longer givens. Sex has become so fraught with anxiety, with rejection signals and fears, with fears about AIDS and safety in general, that just relaxing into it and enjoying the attraction between two ready-for-it guys has become difficult. So your ability to invite intimacy (and control aspects that keep it from happening) is very important.

Sometimes you can do this easily. There is a certain amount of attraction at work, the two of you are well setup for something to happen, and for the stars and nature to take their course.

But other times you don't feel like this is happening. Meeting someone, even after a hot run on the Internet or on the phone, becomes disappointing, scary, and hazardous.

You're sure that what you want to happen is not going to, because he's just *not* in your league. He's too good-looking, too sure of himself, too favored by all of those things that you are sure are never going to land on you. Or have stopped landing.

Anyway, that is what the next chapter is about.

27 Another Handy Concept: No Man Is Out of Your League, But Some Men Are Out of Your Circumstances

"Hope is a bad supper that makes a good breakfast."

Henry Fielding, *Tom Jones*

No man is out of your league, but some men *are* out of your circumstances. Not everyone is as open to new experiences as you are, as curious about other people, as unafraid as you would certainly like to be, or as capable of making other men feel accepted. Why this is so, you can't address. It may have to do with the bitterness left over from his growing up, from his own struggles with himself, from any unhappiness he has held onto within his life. Within reason, everyone is a *potential* partner for you. Only a dope would open this up to the whole universe, but as you get older you may realize that there is a lot bigger playing field out there than you could ever imagine. But not everyone finds himself in the same more open, accepting, and trusting circumstances that you, hopefully, are—*hopefully* should be in, after reading this book.

As in my chapter about rejection, this may seem to some guys like only one of a number of rationalizations to keep you from being deflated when the big ugly reject monster rears its head, and I can see some of you "tsk-tsking." But it is the truth. Although we live in the culture of rejection where "reject" becomes a reflex, circumstances go beyond culture. They have always been there. Some men are simply more open, warm, and inviting than others. You will find them, and the nice thing is being able to recognize them, even past the colder crust that, unfortunately, some of them have adapted for protection. It's up to you, within the art of seduction, to be open to and understand this.

You can do so by trying to see what his circumstances are and trying to fit your own to them, if you find him worthwhile. His cold shoulder may be a transitory defense that he immediately goes into, or it may be permanent.

Here I'd like to go back to what I call the "unbidden gift," something that is unasked for but offered freely. In olden days, unbidden gifts were considered signs of breeding, grace, and goodness. They were the mark of a gentleman. They denoted class. We were not yet in the "got-you-sucker" era of human history, and a gracious offering of unbidden gifts proclaimed this.

What nice part of himself *does* he allow you to see? What piece of his goodness is he sharing with you? What part of his heart is he offering, unbidden, without you even asking?

These unbidden gifts are often real evidences of "circumstance" sometimes even acting against itself. By offering them, he is saying that his own natural goodness is operating even beyond his own ability to deal with you.

Recognize these unbidden gifts. And they will be accepted beautifully, seriously. Within the art of seduction, offer them yourself. Show that you can be open to him, and open to the excitement of the two of you together.

Another unbidden gift:

The fact that he's looking at you and genuinely smiling, even though he may not be saying the most brilliant or charming things in the world. He may not even know how to act "nice" at that moment.

After all, "nice" has become for many men a business ploy. They pour "nice" on for clients and their bosses at work. Now that he can loosen up a bit, let his office defenses down a tad, and not have to put on his mechanical charm, he may be feeling really good about what's going on, even though he may come off as kind of a *schmuck*.

So here your own unbidden gift may be just to overlook that.

It's easy to see the very practiced "image sell" going on around us: exactly what he looks like down to the last hair. But how he's feeling and what circumstances brought him to feel like this are difficult to see. Being able to have any understanding of a guy's circumstances is very important in the art of seduction, especially if the markers for those circumstances are not always obvious. Circumstances, for instance, have a lot to do with behavior: the fact that he's acting like a jerk, being brusque and ridiculous, acting cold. Although he is "in your league" (whether he knows it or not), at the moment he's definitely not in your circumstances. He's not in control of himself, he's not had real intimacy with himself that can give him the security and support he needs. So it may be time for you to move on past him, without feeling hurt or burned in the process.

WORK FOR YOU: Make a detailed assessment of your circumstances right now. How are you feeling? How are you coping with the ideas in this book, and with what's going on in your life? Keep that assessment, and look at it a month after you've finished *The Manly Art of Seduction*. Then look at it six months after. How have your circumstances changed? Whom have you chosen to allow to come in and change them?

_____

_____

_____

_____

_____

_____

_____

_____

_____

28 Dressing for Seduction

"Why don't you . . . fit your clothes easily? Only the English and Americans have this mania for snappy tightness."

Diana Vreeland in *Harper's Bazaar*

A lot of guys have this idea that if they dress so hot that the floor melts under them, that's seductive. Actually, it often results in the opposite. It shows other men that you are so into yourself and so impressed with what you've got that they'd better not apply for the job. A huge number of molten hot guys go home alone. And they stay alone. These guys may do well in instant sex situations, such as sex clubs, the baths, sex parties, etc., but even there they project the image "Look. Don't touch."

I'm sure you've encountered them yourself. They are professional hotties, and even though they may be Einstein brilliant (OK, who am I kidding?) most men automatically assume they're airheads. They may have the muscles, pecs, ass, chest, and dick of death, but the person who takes the most advantage of it is unofficially called Mr. Mirror. Because it seems that they spend so much time in front of him.

If you have an idea that the perfect seduction package for you includes a T-shirt so tight it looks airbrushed on, a pair of 501s that show off every anatomical detail of your crotch, or a frayed jockstrap positioned at exactly the right angle, you might want to think again. Dressing for seduction shows not exactly what you've got, but that you are approachable.

Not porn-star ready, but approachable.

Instead of a Superman tight "T" or polo shirt, a softer, more touchable-looking shirt left open several buttons from the throat (down toward the chest, but not showing everything, at least not until he gets closer) is better. It says, "I'm showing you just enough to make you interested. And the fact I'm a little unbuttoned is an invitation for you to finish the job."

If you want to be a bit coy, a spanking-clean, really white T-shirt under the unbuttoned shirt can also be a turn-on. It means you are showing a freshness that most guys would love to get their hands on.

A sweater can also be nice, especially if it's worn directly over a T-shirt or over nothing at all, if you're of that nature. There is something very animal about that. Like leather, wool has an appeal to many senses: touch, smell, sight.

Going further down, pants should not be skin-tight, but should have a softer, more inviting "drape" to them. Jeans are seductive, but not if you look like you've stuffed yourself into them. You don't need to look like some needy kid who must be the center of attention. Look like you're in control of yourself, and want other men to be interested in you—but not everybody; you should draw the attention of the person you're interested in.

When I was younger, I was extremely impressed with Audrey Hepburn, Ingrid Bergman, Monty Cliff, and Cary Grant. They had what I called "shy glamour." No matter where they were, you were drawn toward them. They were the models for what I wanted to be as a young Southern boy in the wilds of New York and later working as an entertainment journalist in Europe. They did not have to jump out at you. One thing I learned about celebrities was that many of them were actually shy which made working with them easier since I understood that. I also saw that under that shyness, they exuded a quality that made you want to get closer to them, even if only on a fantasy level.

Dressing seductively does the same thing. It shows that you are approachable, have retained your own sense of mystery, and you are not hiding that from others. You are slightly removed, yet at the same time encouraging someone to approach you.

Other seductive items you can use:

Wearing a soft sportsjacket, blazer, or leather jacket with something unexpected under it (a sleeveless T, a light sweater, a shirt unbuttoned enough to show off a simple piece of gold jewelry mostly hidden from view). Don't confuse this with the Miami beach "show-em-the-bare-chest-and-ten-miles-of-gold-chain" look. That got too tired too fast.

A leather band on your bare upper arm, or a simple leather thong tied around your neck. Natural things, like seashells, seeds, or polished stones worn in a neckpiece bring men to you.

A birthstone earring. An antique watch. A really nice bracelet that calls attention to your hand or forearm. Any piece of jewelry or clothing that has a story to it, but nothing so extreme that it takes attention away from you, instead of drawing attention toward you. If you're pierced in sixty places, it may be too much. Leave some of your body jewelry at home. It says you are more interested in yourself than in him.

A pair of loafers with no socks. Bare feet (and ankles) if you have nice feet (more on grooming later) are always seductive. A pair of socks that are totally unexpected if suddenly seen, can also be great icebreakers. (Orange-glow or canary yellow socks in a dark bar can be really nice. With dark shoes, it shows that you have a neat sense of humor: always seductive.)

If you're into leather, use it, but don't look like you're going to find someone, take him home, and tie him up. Leather can be seductive or intimidating. How you use it is up to you, but remember that a huge number of white-hot leather boys go home alone because, like too many other fashion queens, they are more interested in everything they've got than in anything you've got.

Here Are Some Turn-offs to Seduction:

Dark glasses, especially deeply smoked ones. They make you appear aloof and menacing, and make other men anxious because they can't see where your attention is focused. They show that you're playing games, and most men are not interested in that.

Coded hankies. I thought they went out with Ronald Reagan, but in some areas they're still considered the "essence of gay." Umpteen pieces were once published about them in queer bar rags, until every color became confused with another; use them for polishing the furniture, but not your act. Ditto for the infamous "key code," or wearing your keys on one side or another to show that you're "dominant" or "submissive." Unless someone is interested in the antique element of it, it shows that you are more interested in your own cutesy queerness than in him. The same goes for men who wear fourteen pieces of rainbow stuff to show that they are in their "gay" mode. It makes men wonder what happens when you take this act off.

Hurricane-level colognes. If for some reason you're still wearing one, dump it in the toilet. It says you're interested in yourself, not anyone else. However, a light scent, one that he'll have to get close to smell, can be enticing.

Earphones. For some guys they've become a fashion accessory. If you have them, keep them out of sight. If you're wearing them, it means you're off limits and not interested.

Anything that tells someone else's story, but not yours. This includes: designer logos all over you; hoards of political buttons (although one at the right time becomes about you and your story, and this can lead him to want to know more about it); a T-shirt meant to offend (my favorite was "Jesus Was a Fag"; who can compete with that?); and anything that says, "I can afford this, and you can't." If you want to wear your entire Gucci, Movado, or Rolex wardrobe at once, fine. But don't expect anyone who's not primarily interested in your bank account to approach you.

From some of the above, you might draw the conclusion that I'm suggesting you come off Lands End bland and Sears serious.

I'm not. Just let men feel that you are approachable, and that approaching you, or being approached by you, will be rewarding.

WORK FOR YOU: What kind of wardrobe do you have, and how does it work for you? Are you still dressing like the world's oldest kid with the backward baseball cap, punked-out jeans with artful rips and safety pins, or an air-brushed T designed to show off your nipple ring? Are you stuck in clothes that make you look old, worn, and scared of being noticed? Men who are terrified of being "hauled out of the closet" have an ingrained fear of even the most natural human vanity. So where do you stand with your clothes? Now is the time to make an assessment, and maybe get help with a closet makeover. One way to do that is to start looking at men's magazines. Another is to start noticing the clothes of men who attract you. What are they wearing, and how can you come up with a look that is comfortable and good for you, too?

WORK SPACE:
List of what I'd like to wear—

_____

_____

_____

_____

_____

_____

_____

_____

_____

_____

Grooming for Seduction

"Meanwhile I went out to the log johns out back and washed from water in the tap which was delightfully cold and made my face tingle, then I drank some of it and it was like cool liquid ice in my stomach and sat there real nice, and I had more."

Jack Kerouac, *The Dharma Bums*

Under it all, what's really important is grooming. (And of course staying healthy, but grooming adds a nice glow to you and makes approaching you even better.) I've already talked about the importance of good oral grooming. But there are other aspects, too. Like making sure that nose hairs and ear hairs are gone. You don't need 'em and with a little effort you can look good.

Also, eyebrows. You don't have to look like a Russian thug from the Kremlin. Eyebrow hairs can be trimmed back with a comb and scissors; or have your barber do it. You can also have your brows shaped by waxing or plucking, often done at a salon that specializes in that, if you are really having problems with them. (Like you have a tendency to look like Alley Oop or Bigfoot. Although I must tell you, some guys are hugely into Moovian-type men—remember Moo, where Alley Oop was from?—and I have been among them at some point.)

In the old days, before *Queer Eye for the Straight Guy* (also known as before complete consumerization of the American male) most men were intimidated by their own vanity, or lack thereof (or lack of balls thereof, depending upon your viewpoint). Doing something like shaping your eyebrows seemed as unlikely as using dinosaur testicles for bowling balls.

Times have changed, for good or ill, and the truth is that looking attractive is . . . well, attractive. And doing so now means that you take pride in yourself and would be delighted if someone else sees it. So, make sure that your barber (or "facialist") completes his job with your ear hairs, if you have them. He may not want to work with your nose, but a small pair of rounded scissors can do the job, or a small electric trimmer specially designed for it. What's important is that you become aware of this. If you have hairs growing on the outside of your nose, which sometimes happens, get rid of them, too. Nair now makes Nair for Men, and that can work well with back and shoulder hair.

I am not an advocate of chest shaving, but if you're starting to look like a chimpanzee there, then you should trim back your chest hair. You can do this easily with an electric beard trimmer. Some men have thick, dark hair on their chests and it looks great. But if yours looks shaggy and apelike, then clip it back.

Using a moisturizer is a good idea, especially in the winter, when your face (especially the area around your nose and under your eyes) can start to look rough, red, and exhausted. There are moisturizers made for men now. Some of them come under the category of "after-shave balms," although these usually have some alcohol in them and should not be used under eye areas. A small amount of eye cream can give your whole face a lift, with a more rested look. Kiehl's, an excellent, gay-friendly brand that I have been using for decades, makes a great Light Nourishing Eye Cream for both men and women that sinks in immediately and works fine. Once you get used to using eye cream, it's one of those things you won't want to do without.

Nails. There's no reason to have dirty, awful nails. If the idea of having a manicure or pedicure leaves you cold, you can still use a nail clipper and nail file on your hands and feet. Feet are sexy. The soles of your feet have more nerve endings than any other part of your body except the head of your penis, so take care of them. This includes using a foot moisturizer if they become winter dry and scaly.

Wearing sandals destroys feet, yet few things make feet look sexier than sandals. If you do wear them, pay extra attention to your feet, to your toenails, to the soles, and your feet in general. Some men sweat a lot through their feet and are extra prone to foot odor. If you are one of them, change your socks more than once a day and use foot powder before putting on your socks.

We live in an age of grooming, thank God, although strangely enough, our awareness of grooming has not made us any more comfortable with our bodies. If anything, the barrage of commercial grooming messages for men often make them feel more insecure. How can they come up to Madison Avenue's level of young, utterly narcissistic, professionally-coached grooming perfection?

The answer is to groom for yourself—that is, the self you'd like to share with someone else. You may not end up looking like a Boss model (who all seem to be six-four and come from the former Yugoslavia: do they clone them there?), but you'll feel confident enough about yourself that your role in seduction is made easier.

Besides using deodorant (and I go for a simple deodorant, not an antiperspirant which simply clogs pores), a moisturizer, and foot powder; besides making sure that you're showered, shaved in all the right places (if that's what you want), trimmed and buffed; you should seriously consider personal hygiene practices. These include making sure that your genitals are clean, and that your foreskin (if you have one) and the area under it are clean. You should also consider anal douching. Do this even if you're not into getting fucked; you never can tell where his fingers might end up, and what cold water that can throw on a hot occasion.

Use a simple rubber "anal syringe," found in most drugstores, and warm water. Stay away from shower-head devices using a length of rubber tubing and extra water pressure. These can be dangerous, and you really don't need them. You don't have to go in for fancy treatments like using a vinegar douche solution. One or two squeezes with the bulb work fine, after you've lubricated the tip with a drop of petroleum jelly or KY. Make sure that you give yourself enough time on the toilet to release what needs to go. In other words, don't rush out after three minutes and find yourself in an embarrassing situation later.

Personal hygiene is utterly important in any form of sex, and it's often the reason why initial sexual connections fizzle out. You meet someone, things are going full steam ahead, and then you hit a more "private area" of his, one that he generally doesn't show his Aunt Sadie from Buffalo, and it's, "Oh, God!"

At this point, the heat freezes. He cannot figure out what's going on, and you're too embarrassed to tell him.

Some men are not so sensitive about "dirt" in these places, but others are completely grossed out by it. How do you tell him that he stinks "down there," when "down there" is still not something you discuss with a (can we use the word?) *stranger*?

It feels like a conundrum, but there are ways to get around this, and make him know, without fear of embarrassment, what you want.

For instance:

Suggest that you shower before sex. If he objects, tell him you find this extremely sexy. Sometimes this can really help "foreskin fear," found in men who simply back off as soon as they see one. Show that foreskin play can be a part of showering, and you'd enjoy doing that. Tell him that you "like foreskins [this may be a white lie, but it works] but in the past I've met some guys who didn't do right by them. Know what I mean?"

He'll smile, because I'm sure he does know what you mean. In fact, a large number of men with foreskins have sworn off other guys with them exactly for this reason.

And some men simply have foreskins that harbor bacteria because the foreskin is too tight for them to pull it back all the way. This condition, known as phimosis, needs to be addressed, often with circumcision, because it can be dangerous to them. (However, suggesting that may be difficult on the first date.)

Use rubbers (prophylactics) for anal sex. If you find that things are messier back there than you'd like, ask him, "Have you ever tried douching? I do it, and I like it."

Whether you are a dedicated top or passionate bottom, douching before sex is always a good idea, because you never can tell what part of someone will end up there: fingers, palms, elbows. Your anus, like the soles of your feet, is extremely sensitive, and anyone who says that he never "lets anyone near that place" is blocking off a great deal of the pleasures of sex.

Sometimes dealing with sexual issues and hygiene issues is too much at one time. If the last one is adding a problem to the first one, wait until you feel more relaxed, and then bring things up this way: "I really enjoyed having sex with you, but I have a problem with a _____." Be specific, but as tactful as you can. Then say: "I'd enjoy it a lot more if you paid attention to that."

This way, he's helping you, he's doing it for you, and he feels that he's still in control here by doing it for you. The real control issue is that you both want to continue having sex, and enjoying it.

About bad breath, as in *his*: "I'd really like to brush my teeth now. Maybe you should, too."

Keep a spare toothbrush for him. For some reason, guys who'd think nothing of sticking their tongues into places at which Aunt Bertha would blanch, cannot share a toothbrush with someone else. It's always

116

good to have a guest toothbrush. And if you're at his house, then ask to use some mouthwash in order to get him to.

Remember, seduction is getting what you want, and getting him to realize that his pleasure will be enhanced by yours. Part of mastering this art is getting him to see that pleasing you is always in his favor, and will get him what he wants as well.

WORK FOR YOU: As you did with a clothes assessment, do a grooming assessment. What really helps is having a full-length mirror and looking at each part of yourself, to become conscious of it. As in learning to touch by touching yourself, you are again using yourself to become more conscious of what needs to be done. A great number of men have phobias about their sex organs. They find it difficult to spend time washing their genitals. If you are one of them, spend some time in the shower enjoying the pleasures of touching yourself, washing your cock and testicles, lathering the area between your genitals and anus, and also soaping out your asshole. Spend some time experiencing the pleasure of doing this. You can also spend time with your feet, fingernails, teeth, and other areas that need attention. You will find that this attention to yourself can be very pleasurable.

30 Seduction for Dinner

"Life is this way, and the rest is window dressing."
Frida Kahlo

There are few things as seductive as inviting a guy over for dinner at your place. But a lot of men are embarrassed by the idea. It stops them in their tracks because:

They don't cook.

Their apartments are a mess.

They are afraid that if he sees the way they live, he'll take the first train, plane, or exit out.

We need to address these problems one by one, and show that the important thing is that you want to have him over for dinner, and he understands this.

I'll begin with your apartment (or house). It does not have to look like the designer rooms in a department store, but it should look good enough that he'll feel comfortable in it, and you'll feel comfortable with him there. The living room doesn't have to look like human habitation has never taken place there. You don't have to hide all the books you read, the magazines, the eight weeks of junk mail (OK, you might want to hide that), and all the crap that people just forget as they go about their busy daily lives.

Straighten up the living room. Vacuum the rug. Dust, even use a mop—but don't drive yourself nuts doing it. Having books, records (if you still listen to records, and everything is not on your iPod), magazines, and other personal possessions out is good. It reveals things about you, and gives him something to notice and talk about.

About "taste" (whatever that means). Don't worry about it. You may be insecure about what your furniture looks like, what's on the walls, etc., and we're talking here about the worst-possible-case scenario, but there are certain elements that trump taste the first time he comes over. Here are some of them:

Fresh flowers. They don't have to come from a pricy florist;

they can come from a supermarket or corner green grocer. You can stick them in a milk bottle, but they should be fresh and the water in them clean. Lots of fresh flowers mean that you care about his coming over. It's an immediate signal.

Intimate lighting. Keep the lighting low and in corners, but not dark. Dark lighting makes people feel anxious. They want to see what's around them, but they don't need to be stunned by the wattage.

Quiet music. Jazz and classical work. If you can't stand either, then just play something soft. Don't make him have to fight the music to feel comfortable.

Offer him something to drink as soon as he gets there. It will make him feel more relaxed. Offer alcohol even if you don't drink. He may not either, but you should offer it.

Change the sheets on your bed. And, by all means, clean your bathroom. That makes a huge impression on anyone. Have fresh towels available, and some flowers in it. He'll smile.

About food: Make it light, easy to deal with, and not something that's going to hang around or keep making appearances throughout the night. A young man once invited me over for a dinner-seduction and served chili loaded with raw onions. Between the farts, belches, and onion breath, all I wanted to do was get the hell out. Reserve meals like that for after another level of intimacy has been reached, but not for a first seductive meal.

Men, generally, like meat, but serve it in small portions since it's heavy. It's easy to cook a steak. Buy a really good one, broil it six or seven minutes on high on each side, and then slice it thin, allowing about five ounces of meat for each of you. You can serve this with a salad, a good, fresh bread, and some *real* mashed potatoes. Use whole potatoes, don't peel; boil, then mash with a good amount of butter. I use a dash of Louisiana hot sauce to add interest, but just a dash. And, of course, offer a little red wine or soda.

If he doesn't eat meat, find out *before* he comes over. Then serve a pasta dish with fresh vegetables. Even if it's defrosted—and there are some good, frozen vegetarian dinners out there—it shows that you care about his food preferences.

Where you eat is not as important as how much proximity you have to each other. If you have a table that seats six, don't put him on one end of it and you way over on the other. Sit next to him. If your apartment has no dining room, and you eat meals in front of your TV, then eat in the living room—but with the TV *off* and the two of you sitting close.

One of the questions in a dinner seduction is who is going to make the first move. Should you wait for him to, or should you do it?

It's your apartment and he may feel out of bounds coming on to you. After all, he's in foreign territory and men are territorial. Try to have some physical contact with him, but not immediately. Don't pounce on him as soon as he comes through the door. Give him a moment to relax in a new space. This is important, because he may be stressed out finding your place—if he's driven there through a strange area or tried public transportation through a part of town he's not familiar with.

Even if he knows you somewhat, and this is not his first time in your home, things have now taken a different twist. Pushing a sexual button too fast can be hurtful.

So when he arrives, don't come to the door undressed. Dress for seduction, but let him know that you are comfortable with him being there, you don't have to rush things, and he should not expect you to.

Some things you might expect include:

Out of sheer nerves, he may say some really stupid things, like:

"Gee, this is nice. I didn't expect you to live in a place like this."

"You read the _____ [any one of your books]. God, how can you?"

"I'm a great cook, so I have to warn you, I'm hard to please!"

He may not understand that you've taken real effort to do this. Perhaps he thinks you're more secure than he is. So he may be tongue-tied about offering compliments.

He may not say anything for a while, or bring in some of his problems from work, which you don't want to hear. Just let that come out for a moment. It's his way of unwinding and putting himself on more familiar ground in an unfamiliar situation.

What you want to do is to proceed not so much on a verbal level as on a physical one. Enjoy the fact that he's now in your home and you are more in control. This can be very pleasurable and delightful for both of you. But it does not give you permission to start acting like a jerk, parading out all of your *crap* ("I had such a hard week at work." "You can't imagine how hard it was doing this!" "I wasn't sure it was worth it, but I'm looking forward to some great sex after dinner!")

Once both of you have established yourselves in each other's presence, you can "expand." Go over to him, touch him lightly, get closer to him at dinner, and forget about doing the dishes afterwards.

Because chances are fairly high that you both want to go to bed. Unless there has been some contractual statement expressed (as in, "I'll come over, but I don't think I'm ready for sex yet"), this is a very nice time to do it. And there should be some clues that show this is what you want, as in: taking your (and his) shoes off. Inviting him to get more comfortable. Getting even closer to him. Kissing him, and if you feel the signals are working, unbuttoning his shirt.

What happens if the signals are all wrong? He is getting colder and you can feel it. You're moving in, and he's moving out.

Ask some questions:

"Are you feeling alright?"

"Does it bother you that I want to touch you?"

"What would make you feel better? I'd like you to feel comfortable."

This last question and statement are beautiful gifts to him. It's saying, "Your feelings are important to me." He may be in a situation where no one *ever* expresses this, where his deeper feelings are made to seem unimportant and of no consequence to anyone, even to himself. So many men are in that situation, both professionally and socially, that your expressing regard for him is a revelation in his life. The question is, is he connected enough to himself to know it?

If he's not, he may be, later. Or he may simply be too stressed to understand it. Like I've said, I believe in the free offering of gifts, that these are signs that something beautiful is happening. But how a gift is accepted is also important. Keep in mind that you are raising his own value in his eyes, and at the same time establishing your value in both your eyes. You are saying, "I'm aware enough to know what's going on, and I hope you are too."

If this last appeal to his comfort does not work, and he remains distant, don't worry about it. Let him have a few more minutes to settle in and relax. Do the dishes for a moment; offer him something else to drink, or coffee. Then see what happens.

If nothing does and you feel that physically he is still, if not rejecting you, then making you feel that any movement toward him is unwelcome, now is the time to open up the situation. Say:

"Is anything bothering you?"

"I was hoping by this time we'd be closer to each other."

"Is there something you feel you'd like to say to me?"

"Is there something else you'd like to do tonight?"

Basically, you're offering him a chance to get things off his chest. If he's still completely bottled up, nothing's coming out, and you can't get him to budge either physically or verbally, then lower the lights, go over to him, and start touching him in a soft, tender, inviting way. Make him feel that you can initiate something without any problems. He doesn't have to, at least this time.

If still nothing happens, and you're getting really frustrated, then thank him for coming over and suggest that you see each other at another time.

Don't slam the door on the situation (or on him, literally), and try to control your frustration (and, perhaps, anger). There are no guarantees here, and it may be that his reluctance toward the bedroom has a deeper foundation than any previous indications he has given you.

He may be very attracted to you, but still recovering from a bad breakup. He may look hotter than fireworks on the Fourth of July, and come from a religious background where sexual repression is set in concrete.

He may also have physical limitations (I will discuss those in the chapter about sexual dysfunction) and be way too embarrassed to mention them. It may be that the energy that got him over to your place, after a bottle of wine, has been overwhelmed by his own sense of unworthiness, guilt, or fears about health issues, such as HIV. There is no telling where his coldness may be coming from, but now you do have a choice of your own to make.

You can try once more to get closer and make him feel that you are not out there to hurt him. You can begin this with a good-bye kiss, and some real closeness. So when the cards are pretty much on the table, ask him:

"Is there something about this situation that makes you feel awkward, or sexually uncomfortable?"

He may come up with "I only want to be friends," at which point you can tell him, honestly: "I'd like that too, but I believe my friendship includes some real physical attraction."

At this point, you are showing that you are a big boy, you can take honesty, and can be honest yourself. He may still make you feel that the only thing he's interested in is getting out of there. In this case, the question is, do you want to see him again, hoping that this friendship may blossom into something else? Sometimes that happens, and the love and attraction that comes out of it can be very intense. More often it doesn't, and you may find yourself feeling more and more frustrated, and realizing that you have reached the very manly limits of even the art of seduction.

WORK FOR YOU: If you have never had anyone over for dinner, plan a dress rehearsal dinner with casual friends, or even coworkers if you feel close enough to them. This will give you the energy and insight to do what is necessary for you to feel good about inviting a man over for a seductive dinner. The rules for most social eating are basically the same: You want people to experience you on a closer level, you want them to feel comfortable, and you want to have some exchange with them. However, in an intimate sexual setting, dinner as a prelude may require a little more discipline and planning. So doing this cold, with no prior experience at all, can be scary.

Don't forget one of the working-and-non-cooking man's greatest allies: take-out. Japanese food works perfectly, as long as it's not raw sushi. It's light, easy to arrange on a plate, and easy to clean up afterward.

Remember my warning about food preferences. For some men, these become part of their own territorialism and they are rigid about it. A man who seems light and flexible will savagely defend his vegetarianian; this can be a deal-breaker to start off with. If he's a meat eater, and you feel that every meal has to have tofu in it, don't foist that on him, either. Find someplace where you both can meet, as in vegiburgers, or small portions of meatless pasta.

CHAPTER 31

Guess Who's Coming for Dinner? *You*

> "The evening was drawing to a close. Before
> Albertine went to bed, there was no time to lose
> if we wished to make peace, to renew our em-
> braces. Neither of us had yet taken the initiative."
> Marcel Proust, *The Captive*

Now welcome to the reverse: you've been invited for dinner at his place.

Again, most of the same rules apply, except that since he's on his own turf, he may feel that it is ungentlemanly for him to make the first move sexually. Why this is so has a lot to do with people's hang-ups, sex phobias, etc. Maybe Mom told him you don't invite a man over and put the moves on him. Some guys have these hang-ups. The thing to do is follow his cues, as far he is giving them to you. The fact that the cues may not be there may mean that he does not know how to give them. A lot of guys are like that. They have no idea how even to suggest that things could get hotter. But he has invited you over, has gone to some trouble for you, and that means he wants to spend time with you. Acknowledge this by thanking him for the invitation and saying something nice about his home, his cooking, and him—and then allow him some moments to adjust to your being there.

Don't hang all over him like Spanish moss. He may want some time to clean up the kitchen, on his own. Offer to help, but don't insist. Give him some moments to (like a good wine) *breathe* around you, if he needs to. Don't make him feel that you're going to swarm all over him like field ticks, just because he's invited you over.

This will also allow him a moment to come back to you, sit close to you, and enjoy the fact that you're in his place but not overwhelming him.

Since you are giving him autonomy in his own space, you can also feel good about the wish that you want to get closer to him. One of the little known but useful rules about relationships is that it is often not what you bring *to* the relationship that's important, as much as what you don't take *out* of it. You don't rob a guy of his sense of privacy, dignity, will, and happiness. You don't knee him in the balls to get your way.

But you do want to show him that your way is good for him, too.

So, as his guest, you're not there to suck the air out of the room, just to enjoy him. And you should start doing that after enough time has passed for him to realize that he's glad you're there. He's relaxed, he feels in control. Now's the time for you to say, "That was really nice. Why don't we become more comfortable?"

You can follow the patterns I set out in the preceding chapter, but you have to be aware that he may still be feeling insecure about many things. He's let a stranger into his place. Is he being judged about the way it looks, the way *he* looks, how he's handling himself? The list can really go on. So you have to make him feel that you're not there just to run out on him, but neither will you overstay your welcome. You want to become sexual with him, and you want to bring him to the point where he'll really enjoy it.

Body language and position is important. If he's standing against a wall talking to you about the stock market, ask him to sit closer to you. If you're sitting on the floor, get him down there with you. Slowly start to stroke his leg, and then his chest. If he's still talking, then try a light kiss on his cheek, then his mouth. He should be getting the idea at this point, and you can certainly continue it by unbuttoning his shirt or easing his shirt out of his pants.

A "How are you feeling?" check-in is an excellent idea at this point.

You are checking up on his feelings, and giving him a moment to let them register. For many men, this is the only time they'll be asked a real question like this in the course of their week. His boss is only interested in his feelings as they concern work; his friends may ask in a bland, casual way. And that's it. But you're now relaxed and in control enough that his feelings are important to you.

This is a time when soft, seductive, light touching and kissing is very beautiful. Unless he gives you the impression that he wants something hot and heavy, save that for the bedroom whose door you hope will start to open soon.

If things are working in that direction, say, "I'd like to go to bed with you." This means you are making this into a direct wish, in which he can take part.

Don't say, "Are you ready for bed?" That makes it his decision, and he may not be ready to make it, although he may say, "I thought you'd never ask," which shows that he's been wanting you to make the decision for a while.

In either case, what he wants to do is address your wish, and what you are is secure enough to state it.

However, you may end up being stonewalled. A lot of men cannot face their lives without ambivalence. They want to go to bed with you, but they're frightened to; they want to be physically intimate with you, but any kind of intimacy scares or bothers them. What you want to achieve through the art of seduction is getting your own wish, and what you want to show is that you are willing to overcome his ambivalence to get it.

But this does not mean that you are willing to be walked over in the process. *Seduction is not an invitation to masochism*, nor an indication that you are a masochist who gets pleasure out of his own pain. You may, under some circumstances, find certain elements of masochism sexually alluring, but you still want to be in control enough that the seduction can happen.

You can begin to ease him out of his ambivalence with some statements and questions:

"I was hoping at this point we'd be a bit closer. Is something bothering you?"

"I'd like to spend some more intimate time with you. Do you think we could try that?"

"I'd like to spend some time with you naked. I think I'm ready to do that. Are you?"

"That was a really wonderful meal. Thanks a lot. It's really nice out here, but maybe we should go into the bedroom for a while."

And, finally:

"Is there something you'd like to tell me, or you're waiting for me to ask?"

If none of this works, and you suddenly feel like you're talking to a log, then, as in the past chapter, it might be time for you to leave. But slowly. You are still in control, and he might see that if he doesn't push things along himself, then the evening will probably end up as much of a disappointment to him as it is to you. Some men have to have this kind of cold water in their faces in order to hit the "alive" button again. As in the previous chapter, stay in control enough to thank him for the evening, and out of courtesy suggest that you get together again, but be clear with yourself that this will happen only if you want it.

WORK FOR YOU: Think of something that you should bring a man who invites you over for dinner. Flowers or a bottle of wine are always nice, but sometimes a book you love, or a some small gift that shows you've given him something you've thought about and spent time on, is even better. My choices here would be some really wonderful shaving cream (not Gillette; maybe Casswell-Massey), or some massage lotion. These establish an intimate connection with you.

WORK SPACE:

List of possible gifts for him:

_____

_____

_____

_____

_____

_____

_____

_____

_____

_____

32 The Special Tonight: Seduction at a Restaurant

I personally feel that seducing a guy at a restaurant adds a lot more stress than is necessary, but some men feel that upon meeting someone the next step is a cozy dinner out. That is, if it actually is "cozy." Your idea of cozy may be his idea of hell, and vice versa. The first problem is picking a restaurant. Who will do it? You may delight in places that are zingy, stylish, loud, and staffed with good-looking waiters who flirt with every customer. He may want someplace quiet, where everything on the menu is a variation on macaroni and cheese. If you are planning this, it's a good idea to ask him what kind of place he'd like to go to, and what kind of place he is comfortable in. He may hate sushi, and find Mexican food a prelude to heartburn. Getting off to the wrong start can destroy your plans for later.

Whatever place you both decide on, you should make reservations. Don't get there and find that they can't seat you and suddenly there are more decisions to make. When you ask for your reservation, state that you'd like a quiet table. One trick that I find works is to explain that this is a "business meeting." In America, where no one has any business wanting quiet and privacy, bringing business into the situation helps. The staff may wink, but it will get you a table that doesn't resemble Grand Central at rush hour.

As in a meal at home, don't overeat. Getting stewed is a great way to have the evening come crashing down around your head. You want to be in control, and direct the evening so that it ends up either at your place or his. Sharing a bottle of wine, if you can handle it, or having a cocktail before dinner and perhaps water during, shouldn't hurt.

A restaurant meal is a great situation to ask him questions and let him talk. You can do this to help his nerves if he is nervous, but it also keeps the conversation on a track that you can direct. However, if you are the one asking the questions, don't expect him to interrupt and suddenly ask you something. He may not feel comfortable doing that. So don't take this as a sign that he is not reciprocating your interest.

You might ask: "Is there something you'd like to ask me?"

If he does ask you something, answer his questions honestly. But remember, this is a first date, leading, you hope, somewhere, to sex. You don't have to give him the Full Monty, explaining things to him way beyond a casual question. Many dates can end up disasters this way, if you go off on a tear about yourself that doesn't stop until he asks for the bill.

Speaking of which, I always suggest that unless there has been some glaring discrepancy in charges, like he's ordered four martinis and you've been abstaining, you should split the bill "like men." I know this is pure sexism, but women are famous for haggling over every dime of the bill; usually men don't. So suggest that you split the bill down the middle.

But before the bill comes, while you're still on dessert, it's time for you to suggest what to do afterward. This should be done as a wish on your part, and not as an opening question.

"I'd really like to spend some time alone with you after this. How can I do that?"

You notice, I did not say, "Is there any chance I can spend some time alone with you afterward?" This puts the decision-making on him, and takes it out of the sphere of sharing with him your feelings and wishes. Feelings and wishes are powerful things, and can be revelatory, much more than simply asking questions. You are saying to him, what I'd really like is that *after* dessert we get to have something that will be the real reward for the evening. This puts you in a position that is secure, naked, and vulnerable all at once. He sees that you can let down your guard to show your wishes, and that you can reveal what you want. For many men this will be an intoxicating revelation, and it may have more kick in it than that first martini.

WORK FOR YOU: Make a list of three restaurants that you feel would be good settings for a seductive meal. Then, think of things you'd like to talk about on first meeting "him" at each of them.

WORK SPACE:

_____

_____

_____

_____

_____

_____

_____

_____

_____

_____

_____

_____

_____

_____

_____

CHAPTER 33

Seduction Within a Relationship

"A fine romance, my good fellow! / You take
romance! I'll take Jell-O!"
Jerome Kern, "A Fine Romance"

One of the most useful and little-used places for seduction is within a relationship, either a long-term one or one that is getting off course. Long-term relationships often turn sexually cold, stale, or simply sexless. But the romantic/sexual element of even a new relationship can end or be postponed indefinitely ("Not tonight, hon, I've got a headache!"), and the bedroom end up the scene of an endless stalemate.

The cause may be exhaustion, stress, or a familiarity that breeds not contempt but boredom. This happens in many, if not most, relationships over time—gay, straight, and indeterminate—but unfortunately, a lot of guys feel when they are going through it that they are the only couple having this problem. Romance, sex, and romantic sex all require a certain amount of cultivation. They don't spring up from nothing. When they are starved for lack of energy, time, and an environment that is right for them, they stop happening.

There is now a whole industry set up to keep straight couples screwing regularly; couples resorts, couples "get reacquainted" vacations, couples cruises, Christian romance for couples counselors, Jewish togetherness training for couples, couples sex education seminars, couples counseling, even porn movies for couples—all created to put the zing back into any marriage.

Many aspects of the "hot couple" industry boil down to two central concepts:

1) Planning to have a moment alone (or as some people call it, a "sacred space") set aside for romance, intimacy, and sex.

2) Communication. That is, letting him know what she wants, letting her know what he wants. And doing this without embarrassment.

Finally, straight couples are starting to deal with one of the most charged, forbidden areas of their sexual lives: creeping censorship. A

131

primness comes into any married life, and with it a coldness. At a certain point, one or the other or both members of a couple start(s) to feel that all the sexiness around sex is just not "responsible," "adult," "moral," or "right" within the holy confines of marriage.

In the old days, this attitude was taken for granted and you had a lot of miserable, sexless couples and a lot of roaming husbands or wives. (I will get into roaming husbands in a later chapter.) Nowadays, people are a little more open, though in fact many people are working too hard to even think of roaming, and the marriages are as hot as "yesterday's mashed potatoes."

So, seduction is coming back to marriage.

This happens to gay couples as well, but strangely enough, for many contemporary gay couples being open about sex, sexual needs, and sexual diversity has become even harder than it has for straight ones. Part of this is the mainstreaming (what I call the "David Sedaris Syndrome") of gay life, where we want to be like other suburban couples, right down to Dave's Gap khakis and button-down shirts.

Admitting that you want more "heat" in your life, something else besides Jell-O on the table, is now considered immature and tasteless. The sexless gay marriage is still fairly much in the closet; men rarely want to talk about it. It brings on a kind of embarrassment too redolent of failure.

But, there are ways to bring sex back into your relationship if this is something you want and your partner is open to it. Sometimes he may be even more bashful about sex within an established, sexless intimacy than he was before you coupled up. That means that you will have to do most of the leading into a situation of real intimacy and candor.

First, set aside a time to really talk about this—with no accusations. Talk about what you'd like, and ask him what he'd like. Try to make the talk fairly general. If you feel that he is embarrassed, then do more of the talking yourself.

"I'd like to have more sex in my life."

"I'd like for us to have sex together."

"I'd like to know how you feel about having sex. Is there something you'd like to do that I should know about?"

Invite him to share his feelings and fantasies about sex with you. He may want to experiment sexually. He might like to try a threesome, or some kinkier byways of sex like bondage, which many men find extremely exciting. He might tell you that what he'd really like to do is have sex outdoors, or while watching a porn movie, or phone sex while wearing leather or a three-piece suit. Allow him to open up without fear of ridicule or criticism.

Then, in a more relaxed period—a weekend, for instance—give yourselves time to explore what you've been talking about. Go to a sex shop, if there's one in your area, or shop online for sex toys, or drive to some secluded, romantic place and experience being there. The point is to let him know that this does not make you afraid, that you are not made insecure by his sexual revelations. You might even want to add some of your own.

This can include trying new sexual positions, new roles, or showing that you are willing to have a new attitude about romance in general and sex in particular.

For many men, being romantic and intimate is difficult. They can accept an emotionally cold buddy relationship, but not the heat of romance, which often seems to come with other emotional strings attached. But in a long-term relationship, romantic intimacy can be necessary, and having it can often keep the relationship going. If you long for romance as well as hot sex, let him know it.

With romantic feelings often come an opening of other feelings, fantasies, and other aspects of intimacy. Invite him to some real cuddling, relaxed meals shared together, quiet moments listening to music or reading books, or picnics outdoors. These can be preludes to sex or something wonderful to enjoy on their own. Either way, they are part of the seductive nature you want to bring back into the relationship.

Seduction After A Fight

TV sitcoms for some time have made jokes about "make-up sex" and how powerful it can be. There is a lot of truth in that; sex is often the "climax" of some very powerful, often pent-up feeling that is finally allowed to come out and be expressed. The "dance between the sexes" often includes hostility being overcome, and hot romantic feelings finally allowed expression. If you've ever watched flamenco dancing, with men and women as rivals and combatants, or seen a hot tango, you get what I mean. Seduction after a conflict can be fantastic.

It can also blow up in your face if your partner feels that he is being used, is not ready for sex, or you're just using it instead of really resolving what's produced the conflict.

Here are some techniques that can help you with this, and keep the conflict from becoming a door-slamming, explosive event.

If he turns away from you, try to touch some natural, neutral part of him, like his arm, elbow, knee, or shoulder. Don't go for his crotch. Let him see that you want to stay "attached" to him in a warm, friendly, and affectionate way.

Draw him closer to you, but don't go into a big hug or kiss. Let him see that his physical feelings are important, and it's also important for you to express your hurt need for closeness with him.

Ask him if you can sit down and talk about what's going on. One of the worst aspects of fighting is the distance that hostile feelings provoke: anger and distance are an ugly, volatile combination.

Ask him to talk to you, and listen to him, genuinely. Allow him to listen to you. He may have things that, as a reflex, he feels he has to get out, but inside he may be listening to you much more than you think. Don't go into a childish reaction if he interrupts you. As part of seduction you can be in control.

When you feel that the problem(s) have been resolved, or are coming to resolution, let go of him. That's right, give him some "air" between you. Tell him how happy you are that you've been able to talk in this warm, close way. Give him credit for doing it. It's not easy for a lot of men whose only role models may be parents who slammed every door, screamed at one another, and kicked every cat, dog, or child along the way to his adulthood. For many men, it takes a lifetime to get past them. You are giving him a chance to do it much faster.

When you feel that things have calmed down, touch him again, very softly, and see if he's moving toward you. If you feel that he is— and he probably is—you might want to consider unbuttoning something on him, like his shirt.

34 Monogamy and Seduction

For some men, having a chapter on monogamy in a book about seduction makes about as much sense as having a chapter on beef stew in a cookbook for vegetarians. Monogamy would appear to be the opposite of seduction, in that seduction is often used to open up the sexual playing field, and monogamy would appear to close it. However, many men now are looking for monogamous partners, and I feel that seduction as a tool can have a powerful place in a monogamous relationship.

First, though, I think it is important for men who are looking for monogamous partners, or partners who are willing or desirous of being monogamous, to look at their priorities.

Many men who are seeking monogamy think of it as being an added attraction to another man's list of attributes. That is, they are looking for a man who is sexually attractive to them, and has the psychological attributes they feel are important, such as wit, kindness, generosity, sportsmanship, warmth, character, etc. (Here you can pick your own desired psychological properties and make your own list, if you are in the monogamy market, or for that matter, in any market.) Class, money, and status may also be thrown into this shopping list of wants. Such men feel that getting "the whole package" is important, but a desire for a monogamous relationship must definitely be on the list.

My own feeling is that, if you are looking for this kind of relationship, monogamy should be elevated much higher. It should be at the top of the list. This doesn't mean that other attributes should be off the list, but realistically, the desire for monogamy should be something that makes another guy so desirable that this produces its own romantic chemistry and allows the rest of the relationship to happen. The fact that he is willing, in fact welcomes, being joined to you exclusively should, indeed, *needs* to add a lot of heat to what is going on between you.

Once you realize this, and pursue it, then monogamy can result in large psychological and even sexual rewards. First, there is a feeling of privacy and intimacy within the relationship that no one else can invade.

He "belongs" to you, and you to him. For some men, that alone is purely fissionable. It is an immense desire that on becoming a reality can be continuously combustible: pure, raw heat. Sexually, romantically, and psychologically, this man is yours and you are his. You have erected a rose-covered fence around the two of you that is at once beautiful to look at, even enviable to some, and strong enough to deal with all the other problems of life—finances that may fall apart, aging, religious differences, your family and/or in-laws, to name only a few. In a monogamous relationship, he is the embodiment of everything you believe you want to happen. As I have said in *How to Survive Your Own Gay Life*, this is a precious wish come true.

However, roses have thorns, and that can be a problem with monogamous relationships. These thorns can include sexual boredom, and the resentment that festers when one partner feels that he is doing all the work to keep the relationship going, or at some point he weakens and feels that temptation is doing an excellent job at seducing *him.*

It is here that seduction really works to keep your monogamous relationship going, just as it worked to produce the relationship in the first place. In other words, you may have to *keep seducing him* to prevent the relationship from going sexually stale, when love itself is no longer enough.

Therefore, if you feel that you want a monogamous relationship, and there are many reasons to feel that way besides purely possessive ones—the fear of sexually transmitted diseases, the desire to raise kids, the need to feel that your home will never be upset by other relationships—then consider seduction as a tool in your relationship. This is just as it would be if you were not monogamous, but it will be focused only on one man.

Here are some ways to keep your monogamous relationship working, and using seduction in it.

1) Make a list of your personality traits and his, including both desired traits and ones you feel are already there. Once you have described these traits, stage a situation where you will be seducing each of these traits, one at a time. If you feel that your partner is commanding and decisive, then play to that trait. If he is warm and soft, teddy-bearish and deliciously sweet, play to that one; artistic and creative, play to that one. You can set up whole scenarios that work on a particular trait—a military scenario, one set in an art studio, etc.; doctor, lawyer, cop, and thief. The important thing is that you are starting to see each other as

a multitude of layered things, rather than static personalities that can quickly become stale.

Desired traits are fantasies also, and you can discuss this with him, rather than simply pop them on him. If you have ever had a huge desire for him to be a butch, leather top, and this is a stretch for him, suggest that he try this, even if in small stages. He can go from being a top in a business suit to one in leather, and you can enjoy these changes as they appear. The important thing is that you don't take seduction scenarios so seriously that they become painful or so lightly that they become pointless.

2) When you feel stress and resentment building up, allow a specific, but relaxed time for seduction.

This is important in any relationship, and I will go into it further in another chapter, but many monogamous relationships blow up because of unvoiced resentments. Some of the heat caused by psychological friction can be used sexually, but don't expect sex to cure basic situations that have caused the friction in the first place. Some of these situations may be cured by giving the two of you "space," either together, away from others, or separately. Just having a little oxygen between the two of you can cause wonders in bringing the fires back. Once you have allowed yourself this "air," you need to work on keeping the sexual connection going again.

3) Keep in mind that sexual energy and the desire for monogamy are two different things. The fact that you desire monogamy does not mean that you are sexually colder than other men, or that your partner is. You can have a wild, hot sex life, but you will be doing this with one other man rather than with a sequence of them. To do this requires work, and a lot of seductive moves on both your parts. It means not censoring any aspect of the two of you where you both are concerned. If he suggests something that you find really "kinky," don't dismiss it. If he trusts you enough to reveal that he finds other men attractive, don't put him down or feel insecure about it. Part of monogamy is that he will trust you with his feelings. One of the worst things two men can do in any relationship is censor one another, and in a monogamous relationship this censorship is asking for trouble.

On the other hand, part of the "sacred space" of a monogamous relationship (and you don't need to be in a monogamous relationship to create this sacred space, but this kind of relationship genuinely encourages it) can be used to dispel things that either partner finds repulsive or hurtful. Therefore, some degree of discretion is called for. If you press on sharing your feelings, fantasies, and desires that your partner may find revolting, you are tearing down a situation rather than creating it. One of the really exquisite (and truthfully, hot) places between the two of you may be a desire for mutual protection that you both have.

Vacations from Monogamy

There are times when no matter how committed you feel you are (or he is), things may unravel. Some men try to keep this from happening by being with a group of other monogamous men, or only with monogamous straight couples, or socializing within a very closed, trusted group of friends, or . . . anyway, they are working hard to keep this from happening. If in spite of this, you suspect (or realize) that he has been "cheating" on you, then don't freak out. Consider that it might be reasonable to chalk this up as a "vacation" from monogamy, which, in reality could actually allow your relationship to continue for a longer period of time. Some monogamous men consider any break in vows of monogamy to be a fatal break in the relationship ("I can't trust him anymore") and their lives become sadly disappointing, leading to a string of failed relationships, or relationships that never come up to their expectations or demands.

Understand that this is part of the normal, rocky course of any committed relationship, and you can get over it (just as he can). Don't entertain any fantasies that other people's couplings are perfect. You can resume the original relationship, including everything good that was within it.

WORH FOR YOU: Would you be interested in a monogamous relationship? Have you fantasized about it, but felt it would be impossible to try for? Did this chapter help you form any opinions or feelings about having one? Write down your responses.

WORH SPACE:

_____

_____

_____

_____

_____

_____

_____

_____

_____

35 Advanced Seduction Techniques: The Jerk, the Snap, and the Whistle

"You know how to whistle, don't you? You just pucker up your lips and blow."
Lauren Bacall to Humphrey Bogart in *Key Largo*

Much of what I've talked about in the previous chapters has placed you, as the seducer, in the role of the nice guy, which is a nice role to be in. Most people want to be taken as nice, and they want to do as much as they can to stay the nice guy. But a very important part of seduction is maintaining your own boundaries, showing that you will not accept abuse, and are secure enough to stay in control.

Here are three important seduction strategies that ask for what I call "the jerk," "the snap," and "the whistle."

The jerk is like a jerk on a leash. You want to show that you are in control, but you are not going to choke anyone. The jerk works nicely after you've received what I refer to as the "FDG" (Fuck-You-Drop-Dead-Go-To-Hell!!!) response.

He is now fully out of control. Perhaps he started out that way. He may be furious at the fact that you've come on to him, that you are directly expressing your wishes and treating him like an adult instead of a sexless kid, as most of his friends and family treat him.

Your response is a definite but not excessive jerk on the leash:

"Sorry. You don't need to speak to me that way."

"I'd like to see you calm down now."

"That is not something I want to hear right now."

In each of these responses, you are telling him, "You've crossed a boundary, and now I want to re-establish it." You are not hurting him, cutting him apart, lecturing to him, acting juvenile and uncaring. You are establishing this with a simple jerk of the leash that holds you to him as much as him to you. Think of it as an emotional tether between two human beings; as out of control as he is, you are willing to stay in control and still care for him.

The "snap" is a release of temper. You are "snapping," but you're not going into a "diva storm." A lot of guys now have this feeling that they have such a "right" to their own feelings that they can lash out at will, and who cares what gets broken in the process? *He* may be one of those things that gets broken, and that is definitely not what you want.

You want to show him that you, too, have a temper, but can control it. You want him to see it, know that it's there, but not feel punched in the stomach by it. You're letting him know that you *are* pissed and *can* show it.

There are many classic example of snap dialogue. For instance:

"You can cut that out right now!"

"That's enough!"

"Don't even think about it!"

"I will not accept that kind of behavior from you."

This last one is a dangerous position to put yourself in. You can sound awfully high and mighty with it. You are showing that he is approaching your "last straw," and you want him to know it. Also, you are putting the situation into a "behavior" category. You are not insulting him, you're simply showing your distaste at his actions, which can include his attitude and way of presenting it; rejecting him is the last thing you want to do. But that is what he is doing to you at the moment.

By snapping, you are showing him that you are pissed off, but you're not going into a storm, and you're definitely *not* scoring points on him. Don't confuse the snap with the finger-popping, "snap-queen" behavior that emerged as a minor art form in some kid circles a few years ago as a means of showing off, being cute, and scoring points. "Snap queenerie" shows him how powerless you are, and you don't want to be powerless.

So this snap allows you to let some temper out and keep your position firm.

What you don't want to end up with, in the jerk or the snap, is a door-slamming situation where one or both of you calls it quits, even if neither of you really feels that way. He's pissed, you're hurt, or vice versa, and it seems like the only way out is an FDG scene. If you *are* the one slamming the door, count to ten, then come back in. Realize that losing it means that you are out of control. And this is the opposite of what the manly art of seduction is about.

The "whistle" is your invitation for him to re-establish communication or contact. It is an extremely important aspect of seduction, so important that sometimes you have to know that a whistle needs allies, or friends. One whistle may not be enough. He may be too hurt to accept the first whistle. Be strong enough to employ a second or third, if necessary.

A whistle can (but does not always have to) include an apology. There are times when he's been an idiot, and no matter how mature it would be for him to offer an apology, he can't do it. You can be sorry that he's feeling bad, but you are not (necessarily) apologetic that he pushed his way past your limits.

Some forms of the whistle are:

On the phone:

"Hi. I'm calling to tell you that I'd really like to speak with you again."

"I'd like to know when we can see each other."

"Hi. I'm sorry that you're hurt. I wish there was something I could do to make you feel better."

In person:

"It's good to see you again. I've really missed you."

"You're looking wonderful. Seeing you has made me feel a lot better."

"I hope we get to talk. I hate it when we're upset with each other."

In a letter or e-mail:

"I'd really like to talk with you about this. Please give me a call."

"Can you tell me what would be a good time to call you, so we can talk?"

The whistle re-establishes contact. It does not settle who was right or wrong. It does not arbitrate, cast blame, or make protestations of innocence. It just says that you feel he is worth the effort to maintain closeness. Don't expect it to solve your problems for you. But it does open the way for contact again, and it keeps alive the possibilities of real seduction.

Some men might say that what you need here is counseling (and this may be true), but often, especially in the early stages of a relationship, he may feel that there isn't enough value in it (and in himself) for him (and you both) to make the effort. The whistle allows you to re-establish contact, to see if counseling is possible or necessary, and show that you take his feelings seriously. For many men, this in itself is a *very* novel thing. Very few people have made them feel this way, and now you can.

Keeping the J., the S., and the W. on Hand

One of the difficulties with the jerk, the snap, and the whistle is keeping them on hand, in your mind, and usable. Too often, in the middle of a stressful situation, you lose sight of them. ("Where was that jerk? I had it in my pocket a minute ago, and now I'm too pissed off to find it!") Now things are really out of control.

With some men (often, unfortunately, called "drama queens") going out of control has become a reflex. To them, they are acting "authentically," being "honest," etc. This is simply manipulative. When you are with them, having the jerk, the snap, and the whistle close in mind is even more important. And I have to admit, having been raised by a *prima drama* mother, I have been lamentably guilty of this in the past.

You might want to reread this chapter and then think about how many times you might have used these three techniques to your advantage— and his as well—and how much heartache they would have saved.

WORK FOR YOU: The jerk, the snap, and the whistle open up a lot of behavior "challenges" from anyone's past. I'm sure you can remember times when they would have come in extremely handy. Make a list of three times when someone went ballistic, and all you could do was either stand and take it or go nuts as well. Then make a list of three times when you were the one going off the deep end. Be honest. All of us have done this, or gone into an alienating, cold, powerless corner of rage and spite where all we wanted to do was react in some way but couldn't. After you have made the list, try to apply, in your mind, how the jerk, the snap, and whistle would have worked, and helped.

WORK SPACE:

_____

_____

_____

_____

_____

_____

_____

_____

_____

36 Seduction and the Disabled

"In bars and elsewhere, we deaf gay people are
invisible. They don't know about our deafness
until they find out from us. Then sometimes they
suddenly make excuses and take off."
> "Patrick" from *Eyes of Desire,
> A Deaf Gay & Lesbian Reader,*
> edited by Raymond Luczak

People, gay and straight, often have two ideas about seduction (and sexuality) and the disabled. Number one, the disabled are saintly, bright, stoic marvels, showing courage and fortitude that most of us don't have, and because of this, they should be above sexuality.

In fact, they should be neutered like pets.

The second is that disability means deformity. The disabled are morally questionable, revolting human beings (as in Shakespeare's archvillain, the murderous hunchback, Richard III), embarrassing at best, shocking at worst, and anyone who willingly consorts with them sexually, unless it is out of desperation or pity, is in their league.

Again, the disabled should be neutered, like pets.

The second attitude is fading faster than the first, although many people from fundamentalist religious backgrounds still have to get over the idea that disability is "God's punishment" one way or another.

Still, disabled men are usually either patronized or ignored.

Two things have helped change this situation. The first is the openness this era has about the body and its problems. My father died of colorectal cancer when I was eleven, back in 1958. At that time, I could not be told that he had died of cancer, especially a cancer situated in the rectum. "Rectum" was a word locked behind three doors in a doctor's office. Now people talk openly about any form of physical ailment, which to me is wonderful.

The second thing is that the disabled themselves no longer stand for the treatment they once got. They want to be out, open, and part of the whole marvelous, often ridiculous human race. This means that sexuality has entered the lives of disabled people who a few decades ago would have been imprisoned in the category called "sexless."

Despite these advances, there are still things to understand about disability and seduction, and they should be brought out plainly.

1) You don't do someone who's disabled a favor by acting seductive with him, by doling out some attention and affection to him, and then walking away. Your attentions should be real and honest, and take into account the fact that his feelings and sensitivities are the normal ones anyone has.

No one likes to be led on.

2) Don't get the idea that he's "easy" because he's disabled, that he should be grateful for any attention you give him, even if he understands that he is a "last resort."

3) Don't feel that he will automatically respond to you because you're coming on to him. He may have the same problems anyone else would have distinguishing your moves toward him. He may be asking: Are these moves honest? Should I reciprocate? Am I attracted to him, and can I give myself time to feel that way?

For some more recently disabled men, this is a really new thing. He may have postponed any feelings about sexuality while dealing with his disability, so the re-advent of sexuality may be a fairly novel situation in his life. Understand that.

Also, we have hierarchies of disabilities, depending upon how visible the disability is. Men with visible disabilities may have problems in our looks-oriented world that men with less visible disabilities don't have. But sometimes, dealing with a disability that is upfront and out there has given them psychological and emotional strengths that men with less visible disabilities, who have to reveal their disability later, don't have.

This strength in itself can be extremely attractive, but don't expect disabled men to always support *you* in dealing with them. There are times when their own strength gives way, and both of you may need some sense of support from the outside.

Luckily, this is much more available today. In my pre-Stonewall youth, when self-hating homosexuals were more the rule than the exception, disabled men were often ridiculed in bars and social settings. Gay bars were supposed to be havens away from the real world of oppression, danger, and violence. Why was the real world of disability entering them?

One of the few exceptions were leather bars. I had several disabled friends who liked leather bars, even though they were not into leather and S & M themselves. Leather bars, in the old days, were often outposts for sexual and social renegades; any man who did not fit into the old stand-and-primp queer bars of the era was welcomed there. The stand-and-primp bars are now Attitude Bars, and disabled men may feel equally ignored in them—but then, so do most guys who have not stunted all of their brains and imaginations.

This leads to the question, what would you find attractive in disabled men? The answer is, the same things you'd find attractive in any other man, with certain complications. Things can get difficult, but they can be dealt with.

The best way is simply with honesty. Say to him, "I've never been with a disabled man before. I may have some problems with it. Can you tell me more about it?"

Honesty itself can be difficult. We are so unused to it, on a personal, emotional level. One thing is our fear of the "offensiveness" of the situation. Men who are disabled and disfigured (i.e., not physically "perfect") present challenges to us. If you have known them for a longer time, then the disfigurement is not so shocking. Still, it may, at various points, resume its ability to bother you.

My first lover was an amputee. He'd lost most of his left leg slightly below the knee, due to a motorcycle accident that happened while he was in the Navy, three months before we met in a gay bar in New York's Greenwich Village. He was wearing a new prosthetic and I saw that he walked with a cane and a pronounced limp. He was ashamed of it. Not until we were out of the bar and on the way to my apartment did he tell me that he had lost a leg. "I hope that does not make a difference to you," he said.

I told him that it didn't, but the truth was it did. I was nineteen, and shocked by it. I was not sure how to deal with it, how to touch it, how to process his disability in a sexual/emotional way. I was crazy about him, as he was about me, but this "thing" seemed to get more and more in the way. Neither of us could talk about it; he was not given any kind of counseling or therapy to deal with it. After a few years, trying not to deal with his disability, he started drinking heavily, and we broke up.

Afterward I realized that what we needed to do was talk about it, without shame, with real candor. But we couldn't. He was only a few years older than I, and the physical body and its complications were still off-limits. You only did this in the dark, and it was hard enough that two men were doing it.

I have had several other friends and boyfriends in the years since then who were disabled, and have learned that being able to talk about it is extremely important. If you are attracted to a disabled man, be open about the fact that some aspects of his disability may bother you. You're not used to them, but you'd like to be. The truth is, he may not be used to them either. Or, psychologically, he may be in a better state to deal with it than you are. Explain to him that he may need to be patient with you. This can be especially true if suddenly you find yourself revolted by it, even while you're still attracted to him. You might want to say:

"I need to tell you that I'm not used to dealing with your disability. I'd like to be able to talk about that with you."

"I'd like to get to know you. I hope my problems dealing with your disability don't bother you. But I'd like to talk about it."

If you are disabled yourself, understand that seducing other men may be something you want to do. It puts you in control, instead of just waiting. My first lover, who was very attractive and had been used to being in the seductive role, approached me. He did not let his disability stop him, even though he was self-conscious about it. But many men feel that being disabled is an automatic rejection, and are frightened of being seductive.

Sometimes it is just difficult. It's difficult to make eye contact with men when you're blind. But blind men can be very tactile, and can have a physical openness about them that other men don't. Deaf men have the problem of communicating with men who don't sign, or whose lips are difficult to read. Many of these communication issues can be resolved when someone really wants to communicate with them. If you are deaf, you can show a hearing man elemental signs; you can use a notepad to write short notes, and explain that he needs to get into the light for you to see his lips.

So many of these are basic communication problems. The question is, do you really want to overcome them?

And the answer is plain. Yes.

If you are disabled, here are some important things to keep in mind in the art of seduction.

Don't hide. Don't stay in the shadows and feel self-conscious, either from natural shyness or shame. Don't let the insensitivity of others hammer you down. Don't be an "attitude queen," and expect that the right man will come along and you'll suddenly soften for him and he'll see the real you. Try to keep as good an attitude as you'd like to have shown to you. Sometimes you may need supportive friends for this, and sometimes you will need to develop your sense of valor and recognize your own strengths. You've *survived* a lot, and in many ways have it "over" many abled people who are barely doing it.

Good grooming is important. You don't have to go the whole *Queer Eye for the Disabled Guy* route, but looking good should be as much a priority for you as for anyone else. A lot of disabled men end up with a body shame so intense they let their grooming go. This can make it impossible to approach anyone who is offended by the smell of you, or the way you look. Don't place that hurdle on yourself. Being disabled, grooming may take more work, but it's very much worth it. It puts you back into contact with your own body, reducing body shame. The fact that you are not self-conscious about your body means that he does not have to be.

Offer to talk about it. "Am I the first disabled guy you've ever met? I know, a lot of men would clam up now, but I like you enough to want to talk about it."

Don't judge him by his friends. There are *schmucks* out there who are insensitive, unkind, not good when it comes to accepting people who are different. Often this is because they cannot accept their own differences, which we all have. If you overhear one of his friends say something stupid, don't believe that he's feeling the same thing.

If he does not warm up to you immediately, if he is nervous, steps away from you, seems unsure of himself, don't lose heart. Try to continue smiling, keeping eye contact, and showing that you are in control. You can expect some nerves on his part, just as you understand how nervous you are yourself.

If you are not disabled, here are some things you should keep in mind while seducing disabled men.

Don't believe, even imaginatively, that you can put yourself in their place. At some point they may have reactions you don't have, and you can't go there just by pretending that you can understand what it's like to be disabled.

Don't patronize them by saying, "I can understand what that feels like." Say, "Can you tell me more what that feels like?" The fact that you are inviting them to be open with you should be honored; don't allow yourself to be used as a whipping boy for an unfeeling, non-disabled world. There should be some care and understanding on both sides.

Tell him what attracts you about him. Be precise. Not just, "I like your attitude," but "I like the way you smile. Your eyes. The way you tell a joke." Every man likes to be complimented, and a compliment that zeros in on his abilities and attractions is always welcome.

Take him to a place where he is comfortable. If standing is difficult for him, take him someplace where you both can sit. If he needs light and/ or quiet to communicate, take him away from the dark and the noise.

Don't allow your friends to prejudge him. Just as his disabled friends may say you'll never understand him, don't allow your friends to say insensitive things about him; this damages the seduction that is happening, and is actually insulting to you. It says that you are not adult enough to be honored for your feelings.

One of the joys of this period of my life, when some conservatives are gloating about the "death of gay culture," while others see us as the perpetrators of everything superficial, immoral, and moronic in the world, is seeing how much gay men are growing up. Being able to bring disability into the atmosphere of seduction is definitely an indication of this, for both disabled and non-disabled men. I feel very positive about this.

WORK FOR YOU: Have you ever been attracted to a disabled man? Did you show your attraction, or did you feel self-conscious about it? In your mind, approach him now, or if you see him again, realize what you can do to validate and move on this attraction. Write down some things that you feel you'd do differently.

_____

_____

_____

_____

_____

_____

If you are disabled: Did this chapter help you to see some things you may be doing to keep yourself away from either seduction or being the object of seduction? Do you put non-disabled men down because you are automatically sure they "don't get it"? Do you need to change your attitude about this? Have you lost out on seductions that you now feel you might have accomplished? Think about these. How honest can you be about yourself, and how can you change yourself if necessary to use the art of seduction? Write your feelings here.

_____

_____

_____

_____

_____

_____

CHAPTER 37

Seduction and Weight

"... like most other humans, I am hungry. But there is more than that. It seems to me that our three basic needs, for food and security and love, are so mixed and mingled and entwined that we cannot think of one without the others. So ... when I write of hunger, I am really writing about love and the hunger for it, and warmth and the love of it and the hunger for it."

M. F. K. Fisher, *The Art of Eating*

We live in a society obsessed with weight. Some of this is a self-control issue, the idea being that being thin shows you are in control of your own appetite, your body, and your life.

None of this is particularly true, as there are numerous thin people with eating disorders, who are gulping mood-altering pills to keep themselves from feeling completely desperate. The subject of weight has been a long time point of contention in the gay community, where youthfulness and thinness are deemed supremely desirable characteristics. Part of this was an aesthetic problem: Gay men, at least publicly, seemed to have just one model of what is attractive: slim young men, often with no body hair.

This situation changed somewhat about twenty-five years ago with the advent of the Bear movement. Bears were guys who looked like "real men," hairy, chesty guys with real stomachs, arms, legs, and butts. Suddenly men who looked like this and desired other men who looked like this didn't have to feel like an alienated, unseen minority anymore.

Along with this came the idea that you no longer had to look like a seventeen-year-old kid for life. Suddenly there was even room in the queer village for bulky men, men with real girth, who sometimes bonded with the Bears, and sometimes went off on their own.

But the situation is not perfect.

A lot of big men still feel left out of the party, despite there being parties for big guys in many cities, and even conventions for them several times a year. They still feel self-conscious, and their admirers often feel that other, average-weight guys look down on them, wondering why they go after larger dudes.

The truth is that big men can be extremely sensuous, handsome, and can exude sexuality, with lots of electricity in it.

So, if you are a big man and you want to be seductive, here are two things you should keep in mind.

1) Don't apologize for your weight, nor constantly draw attention to it by putting yourself or other big men down when a man is after you. By doing this, you're putting him down as well. Enjoy your own value; he is.

2) Grooming is important, especially if you tend to sweat, and some big men do. A lot of Bear-butch movement guys have this idea that man sweat is sexy. *Fresh* sweat certainly is, but when it's been on your body long enough, the sexiness of it may be in dispute. Don't expect to draw him to you if he can't stand the way you smell. And don't try to cover it up with a cologne that can knock over a brick. In the summer, brief showers twice a day work. In the winter, before you go out hit the water again. If you like to eat, make sure your breath is fresh and your skin is that way, too. If you're fond of garlic, it will be exuded in your perspiration, so watch that.

Positives:

Don't wear only black, unless you want to look (as one heavy man told me) "like an approaching hearse." Some colors look really beautiful on big men, like dark blues, deeper reds, and many greens. Bigger men often have very good skin, without the parched, starved look of many thin men. Don't be afraid to show some of it, especially your arms, and even your legs if you have good legs. Some big men are terrified of wearing shorts, or even short-sleeved shirts. So they go for the Elizabeth Taylor in a muumuu look. You can look really sexy, so why not show it?

A lot of heavy men look good in a short beard, so consider wearing one. It draws attention to your face, neck, and upper body. But don't overdo it. A big man with a really big beard can be a turnoff, except to someone specifically excited by this.

Negatives:

If you have a big, aggressive, outgoing personality to match your size, you might want to tone this down. It can overwhelm men who may be interested in you but feel that they cannot compete. You can let more of this out at another point, if you find this attracts him as well.

A lot of men, regular-sized and otherwise, are attracted to big men because they find them warmer, more engaging, cuddlier, and just plain sexy. Don't be afraid of showing your natural warmth. Don't try to be hard-edged, cool, full of attitude, and off-putting because that's what you feel the environment around you is throwing off, and you have picked up on its rejection vibes. Show that, as a big guy, you can also be a big person, or, as they say, "jovial," in the nature of Jove, the generous and sexually-generous king of the Roman gods.

If you are interested in big men, here are some things for you to keep in mind:

You may have to go over to him. Just because he's bigger than you does not mean that he's automatically aggressive, or that he has got over the embarrassment many larger men feel in a thin-oriented society.

Don't feel that he has to automatically like you because you are not big. He may feel more comfortable and secure with other big guys. Some big men like "chubby chasers" (men who strictly go after big men); others are offended by them. So, announcing yourself as a chubby chaser may not always work. Let him feel that there are things about him that you really like, and his size may be only one of them.

If you have friends who are jerks, distance yourself from them. They may not be sensitive to other people's feelings, but you can show that *you* understand if he feels embarrassed by something callous said in his presence. On the other hand, a big man may feel "at least we've got *that* out in the open," and take any jokes or offhand remarks about size with good humor.

A lot of big men are great cooks, and love to be told that. Be effusive about his cooking. But don't feel that you have to eat like he does. Eating is a personal thing. You may not want to eat everything he does, but don't make him feel self conscious about having a bigger appetite.

Don't tell him, "I can eat all I want to, and never get fat." Being overweight may pose real difficulties for him, no matter how well-adjusted he seems. And don't try to force him onto a diet, or to exercise, although exercising together can be a good idea.

On a practical note:

Sex with big guys can be firecracker hot, but if he outweighs you by a hundred pounds (and I have been in that situation), it may not be a thrill to have him on top of you for very long. Be honest about that. Also, a lot of big men are big snorers. If this is a problem, try to be honest about it, but diplomatic.

An important note about honesty:

In any situation regarding the art of seduction, diplomacy and honesty are important. What you don't want to do is end up bailing out of a twosome because of resentment, the feeling that you cannot be honest, for any number of reasons. These include fear of hurting his feelings while stepping on your own; a family history in which any form of honesty is punished (in my own Southern Jewish family, I had no idea how even to approach honesty; it simply was never practiced in any form); and holding yourself to a formality that takes the place of genuine courage. I have found that the more honest you are, the closer a relationship becomes, even if it's a relationship of a short duration. On the other hand, realize that often what we think of as "honesty" can be used as a weapon, too. Don't use it as such.

WORK FOR YOU: In this chapter I have talked about honesty in the context of seduction and heavy guys. List three situations in which you have felt that honesty was lacking, either from you or another man. You can use the man's name, or code each situation by something you remember about it. Now, think of how you could have brought honesty into the situation, without it becoming a weapon.

WORK SPACE:

Your list—

_____

_____

_____

_____

_____

_____

Also: Have you ever fantasized about big men, but felt too self-conscious to approach one sexually? If you are a big man, have you ever felt self-conscious about being seductive or sexually aggressive?

Write about your feelings on these topics—

_____

_____

_____

_____

_____

_____

38

Race and Seduction: Nobody Likes To Be Stereotyped, or Talked Down To

> "From here you see the whole world / differently:
> brownskin, / tufts of black grass.
> And many times I have given myself /
> to summits like these."
> Melvin Dixon, "Getting Your Rocks Off"

Fools rush in where wise men fear to tread, and in this chapter I am probably in that category. Race is still an extremely sensitive area in American life, and in much of the world for that matter. In my lifetime, I have seen segregated drinking fountains at the Sears in Savannah, Georgia, where I grew up, and five decades later, an African-American president of the United States. We have had huge changes, but race is still a powerful divider of people in many other places.

The issue of race has also meant that some men who want to cross race lines seductively still find themselves inhibited about doing it. Much of this can be attributed to that fact that in America, still very much a white country, what is considered "normal" is often what is seen, characteristically, as "white." This means that white men often have stereotypes of men of other races, while in truth stereotyping goes in all directions.

So, men make up their minds about the characteristics of other men, what they are or should be, before they've actually dealt with them.

One thing that we often forget in the larger race issue is that race itself, as understood through skin color and other characteristics, is vastly redefined through culture and class. Any of your stereotypes about someone of another race can quickly be thrown out the window, once you start to see a larger picture of him because of his cultural background, class background, educational background, and his real character.

Meeting men and seducing them is nerve wracking enough, under the best circumstances. So, it's easy to fall into stereotypic thinking. One aspect of stereotypic thinking is that you know everything about your own race, class, and culture, and he knows nothing about this. Therefore, after stereotyping him (and yourself), it's easy to talk down to him.

The other approach is that you *think* you know everything about *his* racial or cultural background, and right off the bat you're going to show him just how much you know, how totally comfortable you are with it (maybe even more so than *he* is!), and even how he *ought* to act as a member of his "tribe."

Once again, you've stereotyped him, and now you're talking down to him.

Here are some things to think about in cross-racial, cross-cultural seductions:

Everyone likes to be treated as special, but not as different. Compliment him on his uniqueness, without making him feel that he is a "perfect representative" of his race or group. My favorite example of this was a man who once told me, quite sincerely, "You're really handsome for a Jew."

Don't be afraid to ask questions. It does not mean that you are now being a dumb white guy, or a naïve Asian. It means that you are secure enough not to have to pretend that you know more than you do.

Realize that shyness comes in all colors. The fact that he does not respond to you does not mean that he is not interested in you because of your race. No matter what your color is, or his, you may be attracted to someone who is not prepared to meet you. Give him a little time to get used to you, before you judge that he is not interested. The best thing to do is to let him know that you are still interested—you are secure enough to be patient and not be offended. He may change his mind.

Do not judge him by his friends. There are a lot of stupid people out there who may say all sorts of dumb things. The fact that he is with them, for whatever reason, does not mean that he is as insensitive as they are.

Some men react to compliments and comments about them (or the weather, for that matter), faster than others. If he is slow to react, that does not mean he's not interested. He may simply be processing the fact that you are talking to him and engaging him.

In a situation that is racially or culturally prone either to sensitivity or questioning (in other words, you feel fairly strange there, for whatever reason) give him a chance to react physically to you. Coming on like gangbusters may offend him, no matter how attracted he is to you. This is especially true with some Middle Eastern or Asian men who are affectionate with each other, but in front of a stranger, may be very inhibited.

Knowledge can be power. It's important to have some cultural reference points, without falling into stereotyping. An example of this is the importance of gifts in some cultures, and the equal importance of recognizing, accepting, or reciprocating them. If you buy him a drink in a bar, expect him to buy you one back, and accept it graciously. Don't insult him by saying, "You didn't have to do that." If he says something nice to you, say something nice back, instead of deflecting it with humility. In some cultures, this is seen as rejecting a compliment, and it is insulting.

If he comes to your house, or you go to his, ask him what would make him feel comfortable: "Am I being too forward with you? I'd like to kiss you, is that all right?"

Sexual roles in some cultures are much more rigid than in American romantic gay culture, where "tops" and "bottoms" trade places, butch linebackers get into drag on Halloween, and today's leather daddy can turn into tomorrow's boy. You might want to ask questions about this before getting into bed. "Is there something you don't like in bed, or will never do?"

This question seems to bother men less than "What do you like to do in bed?" which puts them on the spot. Some men are verbally inhibited about this, but they will point to something and tell you, "No."

Words, and how they are used, change by culture. The fact that you are his "friend" may mean more to him that the fact that he is your "boyfriend" or even "lover." The category and definition of friendship may have huge value to him, and he may not bestow it easily, if at all. So, respect that you are his intimate "friend," and don't demand that he define you in some way he may not be able to.

In many cultures, "family" which can include close friends is extremely powerful. He may want you to meet his "family" right off the bat, even before you have sex. Consider this a normal thing, and not a test. Realize that the "outness" of American gay men may seem foreign to him, and as a concept not worth trading for the closeness of family or an extended clan that does not understand him as being gay. In his world you are a *friend* to be accepted as "family," not his *lover*, *partner*, or *spouse*.

If you are crossing racial or cultural lines, realize that shyness comes in all colors, including white. Don't feel that he is being racist if he does not jump toward you, or that someone who seems much colder than you

158

expected, or suddenly grows colder after some time has gone by, is being stand-offish. It may be that after the initial excitement has cooled, a man reverts to his own characteristic shyness.

You can help this situation by saying, "I understand. I can be shy myself sometimes." The idea that you are attempting to understand him can be very helpful. But give him some room and space to figure you out. As I said in the initial chapters, seduction requires a certain amount of "air" for it to work nicely. Without it, seduction becomes threatening and choking. In cross-racial and cross-cultural seductions, this "choking" experience can be painful and difficult. What you want to do is give both of you a chance and place to really look at one another, and smile. On paper, this sounds easy, but in real life I'm sure you know how difficult that can be.

WORK FOR YOU: Think about times when you have been wrong about men, and can now see that. Assumptions can be particularly killing in cross-racial/cultural seductions, but we cling to them often even when attempting to approach men who mirror us. Seeing and throwing out assumptions show that you can be open to the possibility of being wrong, and open yourself further to successful seductions.

Write down some assumptions you have about men regarding race or culture. If this is too hard to do, simply list any assumptions you have and be conscious of them.

WORK SPACE:

_____

_____

_____

_____

_____

_____

_____

_____

_____

_____

_____

_____

39

Class and Seduction: Sometimes an Even More Charged Situation

"'Allen, I was *what* they call a *ginzo*, know what
I mean? . . . Poor white trash immigrant types,
just ripe for that ol' American dream. And I was
a queer who didn't like, let's just say, your other
type of queer men. You know, New York pretty
boys who think they're so hot-shit cool.'
'Yeah, sure.' About them, I did know."

Perry Brass, *Warlock, A Novel of Possession*

Class is one of the great unspoken taboos in seductive behavior. People
have been crossing class lines sexually for a very long time, at least back to
the Bible, and certainly back to D. H. Lawrence's Lady Chatterley cavort-
ing with Mellors, the earthy gamekeeper. E. M. Forster's Maurice stole off
to the greenwood with a gamekeeper of his own. Sometimes class can be an
even more charged and difficult situation than race or culture, because we
don't like to admit it. In America's ostensibly "classless" society, admitting
that someone comes from another class can be particularly difficult.

Mostly, what we try to do is find polite ways to edge around it.

This may be made even worse when both men come from the same
racial or cultural background, so that dealing with class becomes a
thorny, invisible issue. Another complication in dealing with class differences is that "class" is not exactly the same thing as money, even
though they're fairly closely linked together.

You may have more money than he does (especially if you've just
made it), but he may see himself as coming from the same class that you
do (or a higher one, if he went to a prep school, has more education, and
aligns himself with the "ruling class"). You may think this is just "snob-
bism" on his part, but it's the way he identifies himself.

Sometimes things are more apparent. He's working-class, and you
aren't. Or vice versa. At a certain point, although you both speak rough-
ly the same English, it means different things to each of you. *What* you
do, *how* you talk, and how you *deal* with things have a class value, and

that's where the situation can get sticky.

In cross-class seductions, keep in mind:

As with race, no one likes to be talked down to. Even worse is someone trying to impress you when you feel that you don't need to be impressed. You may be sensitive enough to realize that his wanting to impress you is complimentary, but it's easy to cross that line where his need to impress you, over and over again, with how much money he's got and where it came from, becomes insulting.

On the other hand, false modesty can be grating. If you invite him back to your fourteen-room house and say, "Oh, this little place. You should see where I grew up. That was big!" don't expect him to do cartwheels. You should be normally, moderately proud of what you've got, because chances are that there are things he'd like to be proud of, and he should not be held back by the imposed false modesty of another class.

Don't make him feel that you're slumming with him, and he's someone you could not possibly introduce to your more "serious" friends, whom you mention constantly to him. Try to be natural with him and his friends, without going through the "puff-up" that wealthier people often do with each other, dropping names, social cues, and not-so-subtle references ("Yes, she just closed up the house in *Bah Hawba*."), as a reflex. The fact that he and his friends don't do this may be what attracts you to him. There is a very natural part of you that wants to be with him, so enjoy that.

On the other hand, make him feel welcome when you are with your friends, and you are speaking in that familiar, intimate language you have with them. This special way of talking and joking exists with all friends, but class differences can make him feel especially locked out.

Don't push him into situations where he is over his head financially, and he should not do the same thing to you in situations where you feel out of place. He may not fit in at a four-star French restaurant, and you may not fit in with some of his drinking friends. At a later point, maybe both of you will feel comfortable in either place, or someplace in the middle.

When you meet him, try to be natural, not stiff, and don't set out to impress. Instead, you want to be impressed by him—no matter what the class situation is. Impressed by the fact that he is someone you find attractive.

Unbidden gifts are very important. The fact that he brings you something of value to him, no matter what its dollar value, is not to be taken lightly. If you are from a higher class than he is, you may find it easier to offer things that he cannot. You may be able to afford more freedom: You can fly away for the weekend; you may not have to worry about what your boss thinks, or that your family knows about you being gay. So if he offers you some piece of his free time and his company, prize it highly.

Be impressed with what impresses him, and do it honestly. Don't condescend to him by showing that what impresses him is really nothing. This might take some real effort on both your sides. For instance, sports may mean nothing to you and everything to him. So try to see sports as another area of performance and expertise, like dance. Pop culture may be something he adores, while you know the plots of two dozen operas. No one needs to throw his own feelings and values away, but simply to see the feelings and values of another. Since you take him seriously, there should be room for him to take you seriously, too. If not, a lot of class resentment can build on both sides.

Don't expect him to understand all of your intentions. He may be much more physically direct, and want and expect this. Saying "The bedroom is over there," may not mean, "We're going to go to bed." On the other hand, any physical overture toward him might be taken as a signal for sex. Otherwise, he may just see you as coy, game-playing, and cock-teasing.

Don't be surprised that he is "really smart." Much of what we call intelligence is based on verbal skill, which in the more middle-class gay world has risen to the stratospheric levels of art (as in big displays of "put-down" art, "impress-you-at-all-costs" art, and "I'm-not-really-listening-to-you" art). The fact that he's not chattering away does not mean he's dumb. He may be getting things a lot faster than you are, even without some of the verbal tools deemed necessary to make it in your world.

You have probably noticed that most of the above deals with more middle-class or upper-class men dating working-class men. If you are on the opposite side of this equation, there are other things to watch out for in this particular dance of seduction.

His time, for better or for worse, may be more valuable economically than yours, just as his expenses are higher. Don't punish him by making him wait for you if he invites you someplace. On the other hand, don't be devalued by his valuable time. He can't just drop you when something more pressing dollar-wise comes along, without an explanation and apology. This is why rich men go through wives so often. At a certain point even the priciest wife gets sick of being set aside for powerful clients, celebrity buddies, etc.

If you feel walked over, let him know it. Use the jerk, the snap, and the whistle. But remember, you only have so many times to use these techniques before all the whistling stops. You don't want to go into a full-fledged, get-it-out-of-your-system atomic explosion. Your buddies may be used to this, but he'll just see this as an invitation to quit.

Don't humiliate him by showing him that his value, whether in dollars or prestige, which he's worked hard to keep up, means nothing to you. He has pride, too. Don't show up at his house for a party looking like you just went camping for three days. He will appreciate your efforts toward him, as much as you should appreciate his understanding of you.

Don't put down the fact that money is important to him, and you, since you've never had it, are *way* above it. He may have just lost his megabucks job and is in total depression about it. Try to understand that, deeply, without being a jerk about it. You may find this a situation with the seduction itself: the first thing he may do is start talking (or even blabbing) about his job, his house, his friends, his money, because he's nervous meeting you and these topics are safety nets for him. You may think him pretentious and phony, when the truth is he's actually terrified, no matter how much moolah he has.

WORK FOR YOU: In my book *How to Survive Your Own Gay Life*, I deal with how money can destroy relationships, and also how it can be used constructively. Think about this and how in your past you might have made mistakes regarding money and class, or done the right things with it, even though these things might have been wrongly interpreted. How will you recognize these situations in the future? List points that you'd like to remember:

WORK SPACE:

_____

_____

_____

_____

_____

_____

_____

_____

_____

_____

40 Penis Size and Seduction

"He had the leprosy of gay men, a small penis."
Andrew Holleran, *Dancer from the Dance*

Since so many gay men get all their sexual cues from porn movies, size has become even more of an obsession in gay life than it was before the world's biggest cocks invaded your DVD player every night. This is not to say that size has not been a "concern," to put it mildly, in the past. When Kenneth Anger in his book *Hollywood Babylon* revealed that Montgomery Cliff was known to several bitchy queens as "Princess Tiny Meat," Cliff was reported to have cried, "Is nothing sacred?"

For some men, size is a constantly inhibiting factor. They feel that their equipment does not come up to Falcon Studios level, or even "normal" dimensions. Many of these men spend their lives in fear of being exposed, ridiculed, or hurt. Sometimes this fear is so inhibiting that sex itself becomes almost impossible, except in the form of phone sex or solitary masturbation. Some men are so ashamed of their penises that they don't want to touch it; even masturbation is out. One man I met was sure he was really born intersexed, that is possessing female genitalia. He was not. He simply had a small penis.

Another man with a small penis told me that he could only be a bottom. "It's ridiculous for me to try to be a top with this." Since he was very successful in business and had an aggressive personality, he became an aggressive bottom, openly going after guys but with the idea that in bed he had to take a certain role.

Several younger men have told me that this has become Standard Operating Procedure, that men with small dicks instantly become bottoms. This is sad, and even stupid, considering that this situation is not based on real sexual feelings, energy, or satisfaction.

In the past, I knew lots of well-endowed guys who were confirmed bottoms, and small guys who were tops. Today when "Image is everything," genitals are determining sexual patterns, instead of the men doing it.

One thing seems real to me: any man who rejects you because of the size of your dick is not using his brain to think with. He's using *his* dick. He's saying that this part of you is more important than the rest of you. It's not. But rejection because of size is hard to deal with, and for men who are used to this type of rejection, being engaged in seduction is difficult. The feeling is, very quickly he'll find out I'm small and be disappointed.

This feeling can become engrained, leading to real sex-phobia. Normal desires for sexual intimacy and warmth become twisted into bitterness, loneliness, and internalized homophobia. You start to feel that "all queers are interested in is size, and I don't have it."

This is definitely not true. Not all men are size queens. In fact, some men really like and desire men with smaller genitals. They find them more fun to handle and play with, aesthetically beautiful, and very sexually satisfying. There can be a kind of coltish boyishness about small cocks (which many straight men find in the opposite sex, to their delight, in "small-chested" girls), and they like that, too. If you are a smaller guy, there are things to keep in mind as you develop your own skills in seduction.

Being small does not mean that you cannot be aggressive. And forget the idea that you can't be a top. Actually, one of the best tops I'd ever met in my life was small; he had me literally hanging off the ceiling, because he was a wonderfully exciting lover. So concentrate on being a wonderful, sensitive lover, as well as being a top.

You can bring up the issue of size at a certain point, so that it is not a "surprise." You can say this as, "I need to tell you, I am a smaller man. I want you to know that, in case it bothers you."

Doing this puts you way ahead of the game, in that it adds to the intimacy of the situation. It says that you value him enough to want to be honest. Most of the time—really, *most*—size should make no difference. If it does, you have spared yourself a situation you should not be in. Don't feel bad when it happens. You can't change yourself, despite huge amounts of bullshit promises about penis enlargement on the Web. But you don't need to be bothered by the limitations of other men's sexual tastes.

If you do feel that you're being cold-shouldered and rejected, then say, "I'm sorry you feel that way. Maybe at some point you'll change your mind." In other words, when he grows up.

One other bit of advice: Learn to enjoy your body. Start going to nude beaches. Get over the fact that you're scared of exposing yourself, because you feel that it will always result in embarrassment. In most nudist situations, you see guys with every sort of endowment and in every kind of physical shape. Body shame has nothing to do with "what you've got," but with how you feel about what you've got. Once you get over your feelings of general body shame and size embarrassment, you'll find responding to men a lot easier, and seduction itself happening.

If you are interested in a smaller guy, here are some things you can do to make things go better for both of you.

Pay affectionate attention to his penis. Make him feel that you are enjoying it, which you are anyway. Neither of you has to hide it, not mention it, or pretend that it is not there because it's smaller.

Question jerks who make him feel bad with small dick jokes (what I call the "race" jokes of the queer world), by asking: "Why do you have to say that? I don't find that funny."

Let him know that you'd like him to call the shots, too. That the fact that he's small does not mean that he has to be apologetic, reticent about sex, and unwilling to initiate sexual activities, especially the kind that he'd like. Be open to talking about size, but not obsessive about it. It needs to be a situation you can talk about, and then put to rest.

Finally, remember: Small is a description, not an indictment. Some of the sexiest men I've ever met have had small equipment, and some of the least attractive men I've met have been large. The real question is, how can you make a small man know he's sexy, if he doesn't already?

WORK FOR YOU: How much is size—your own and other men's— an issue for you? What do you need to do to change that?

Make a list of five men you've known sexually. Did the size of their cocks change your feelings about them? Did it make you want to be with them more, or less, and for how long? Many large guys will tell you that just having their equipment does not keep other men around, and they learn this in spades.

On the other hand, have small men made *you* feel bad because of the size of their endowment? Did you feel punished by them obsessively pointing out what they lacked, making you feel guilty about it? If you are small and size has been an issue has this chapter been helpful? Can you list things that you wish I had covered? Even more important, what have you learned that can be of help in the future?

WORK SPACE:

Your list—

_____

_____

_____

_____

_____

Your feelings about size—

_____

_____

_____

_____

_____

CHAPTER 41 Sexual Dysfunction and Seduction

> "To make matters worse: I am, perhaps from fear
> or nerves, or maybe even a cruel trick of hered-
> ity . . . prone to impotence. Or, in TV lingo, 'erec-
> tile dysfunction.' I can get 'junior' up, nudging
> him cautiously awake, then with no warning, he
> stops paying attention. He (okay, *it*) goes limp.
> Numb even. Like it's only an extra piece of flesh
> down there where my stomach ends."
>
> Perry Brass, *Warlock, A Novel of Possession*

Sexual dysfunction is a problem many men are experiencing. It generally has two forms: premature ejaculation and erectile dysfunction. Premature ejaculation usually affects younger men and is fairly easy to deal with. If you experience premature ejaculation, a simple technique called the "squeeze technique" is helpful. If you feel close to ejaculating, squeeze the underside of the head of your penis. This forces blood out of the head, and lowers your erection. Do this gently, and not too often. You can end up with a sore penis if you overdo it.

Erectile dysfunction (ED) is the inability to achieve and/or maintain an erection ("hard-on"). In the past men were starting to experience ED in their mid-forties or fifties. Now this is happening in their thirties and sometimes even in their twenties. Often this is due to stress. Other factors that can lead to erectile dysfunction include:

Drug use, either from prescription drugs such as tranquilizers and antidepressants, or street drugs such as forms of amphetamines, poppers, and downers. Some cold medicines and antihistamines have been known to cause temporary sexual dysfunction.

A history of extreme sexual repression, coming from conservative religious, sex-phobic "training" at home or at church, taunts and violence at school or work, sexual violence such as rape, and severely internalized homophobia or sex-phobia.

Age is a factor in sexual dysfunction, but often age is increased as a factor with other psychological problems as well. These can include:

a general lowering of self-esteem following financial or professional problems (especially found after men have been fired); nervousness and anxiety over sex, sexual performance, attractiveness, and self-image; as well as drugs you were prescribed for heart problems, diabetes, and pain relief.

Diseases like diabetes and HIV can have side effects of sexual dysfunction, either from organic physical causes, or from drug side effects. If you are taking drugs for these problems, ask your doctor about the sexual side effects. Some men are shy about doing this, but it is important to have a doctor you can talk to about sexual side effects as well as other sexual problems.

Injuries and operations. These can include spinal problems, trauma to your genitals, and even some forms of aftershock (Post Traumatic Stress Syndrome) from accidents or other violent events.

If you do think that your dysfunction has a physical origin, it's possible to get this diagnosed with an MRI of your penis. Many urologists can do this now. They can also examine your penis erect with an injection of a drug like Prostaglandin E1 or Phenotolamine into your penis, enabling the urologist to examine the veins and capillaries that cause erection, to see if any of them are blocked or injured.

There are many ways to deal with erectile dysfunction. In fact, it's hard not to know about them, since for a while Viagra was the most prescribed drug in the world. There are now about half a dozen competitors; your doctor may be able to prescribe one that works well for you. The main competitor is called Cialis, "the weekend drug," because it works over a longer period of time, with a full duration rate of up to six hours and some effectiveness for up to thirty-six hours.

The clinical name for these drugs is phosphodiesterase (PDE-5) inhibitors. Never mix drugs prescribed for erectile dysfunction with nitrate drugs such as poppers, or any form of amyl or butyl nitrate. Doing so can cause an instant drop in your blood pressure, which can be fatal. So keep the "Never mix, never bother!" attitude seriously in mind here. And if you know anyone who is doing this, be kind enough to warn him about it *seriously*.

There Are Some Techniques and Aids Helpful with Erectile Dysfunction

Cock rings can be very helpful. The best ones snap off and can be adjusted for size. One that is too tight can injure blood vessels. Some men like the sexy feel of big metallic cock rings. Other men like more high-tech gizmos such as vibrating cock rings, or ones that come with studs or buckles. Some cock rings are also parts of halters for leather S & M play. Basically they all do the same thing: keep the blood flowing into your penis right there, strengthening an erection.

For some men, a good technique is to sit with their back to their partner, between his legs, and have him play with their penises manually, softly getting them to erection and then beyond. This takes some of the "competition-anxiety" out of sex: You can't see his erection, and you're not touching your penis, so some of the sex-phobic internalization has stopped. Also, if some of your problem comes from being taught that masturbation (and other forms of sex) is wrong, you're not the one doing it.

Sex games which take some of the personal responsibility out of sex can be helpful—a least for a while, or to start. These include sex with a masked or hooded man (you can't see his face, so no one is witnessing your embarrassment); wearing a blindfold yourself (so that sex becomes totally tactile); or being with someone else who is blindfolded (again, you don't feel you're being watched).

A useful, but time-consuming technique is called "sensate focus," developed in the 1970s by Masters and Johnson. The purpose of sensate focus is to guide the man with erectile problems to focus on the physical aspects of sex, rather than psychological ones. The primary idea at work is to "get out of your head and into your body," so all the past mental images and techniques once associated with erectile problems, such as heavy masturbation fantasies, porn, anonymous phone sex, etc. are avoided. Sensate focus is broken up into several activities. During the first sessions you and your partner will only lie with each other, "spoon position" and synchronize breathing, taking long slow breaths together. You will follow this by touching and stroking each other every place except genitally. The idea is to associate touching with everything *but* erection, so that erection anxiety is avoided. Erection is not the goal, simply tactile pleasure.

This can be an extremely bonding situation for many men who've never had any physical connection without erection fears. After you have focused on non-genital touching for several weeks, you can touch genitals. Focus on the partner with erectile problem's penis, but always with the idea that any kind of erectile response is good, no matter how fleeting. You can also practice some of the techniques I gave you in Chapter Twenty-One: Nine Very Seductive Activities

You Should Try, as well as what I call "mouth teasing"—placing the soft penis of your partner close to your mouth, then softly caressing and licking it while he touches his penis and allows it to get as hard as it will.

Do this several times until you encourage him to place his penis in your mouth. The idea of sensate focus to is relieve sexual anxiety until sex and erection naturally come together. It does not work all the time, but can be effective even if to move sex out of an area of anxiety into a more comfortable one of not worrying about erection. Later, it can be combined with a medicine like Viagra.

Seeing a sex therapist can be very helpful. Many larger cities have sex therapists who work with gay men, and some massage therapists do sex therapy as well, although this becomes an "iffy" situation since massage therapists are easily busted by the police as "prostitutes" when they offer any service involving sex. Sometimes a regular therapist, especially a gay one or one with many gay clients, can recommend a sex therapist, and some urologists work with sex therapists. Your urologist's attitude about sex is important. Many urologists are conservative, sex-phobic and homophobic, considering that they specialize in problems of the sexual organs. You can find out more about sex therapists through the American Association of Sexuality Educators, Counselors and Therapists (AASECT), a non-profit, professional group for sexuality counselors and sex therapists, which can be useful for finding a sex therapist.

TV ads promise universal sexual success, youthfulness, and happiness if you use their product. One of the challenges of erectile problems they don't go into is separating your problem from the man you're with so he doesn't feel that he's responsible for it, and you don't make him feel that he's part of the let-down if you can't stay hard or climax. Some non-dysfunctional partners automatically feel, "I didn't do the right thing, maybe I should have tried harder." Or, "Now he just wants to get rid of me because he can't cum."

If you have sexual dysfunction, it is a good idea to let someone know fairly soon in the seduction process, to avoid embarrassing you or confusing him. Some men feel that if you cannot get an instant erection, you're not really attracted to them. Then they feel rejected, and want to leave. So letting this out and into the open prepares both of you. You can do this by saying:

"I think I need to explain to you that sometimes I have erectile problems. It has nothing to do with you. I'm really attracted to you, but I thought you should know this."

Or: "Sometimes I fail to achieve an orgasm [you can also use the terms "climax," or "cum"]. That doesn't mean that I'm not having a good time, or didn't like what was happening, or that I've lost interest. A lot of guys don't understand this, but I hope you will."

You should also time your drugs for dysfunction. Viagra works optimally taken on an empty stomach, about half an hour to ninety minutes before sex play. Levitra and Cialis are not affected by food, although the general feeling about these drugs is that they are not as intense as Viagra.

Other helpful hints for men dealing with sexual or erectile dysfunction, either in themselves or their partners, include the following:

Make putting on a cock ring and the waiting time for drugs to kick in part of foreplay. You don't have to hide from one another until all systems are go.

Erectile dysfunction drugs have little effect on climaxing; they can help with an erection, but not a climax. If he has a difficult time climaxing and you don't, you might want to climax earlier and then wait until things heat up again, in, say, forty-five minutes, for instance, and then work toward him climaxing. If you can, delay your climax until he is close to his. What you don't want to do is climax, and then jump up to go home: this is really poor behavior for anyone.

Understand that if he cannot climax, it is a difficult situation for him. Don't dismiss it. Encourage him to climax on his own, either alone later by masturbating, or with you there. If he does masturbate with you there, ask him what he'd like you to do—this can range from you touching and holding him to taking a very active role in his climax.

Let him tell you what he'd like to get out of sex. This could be a huge amount of kissing, cuddling, and sucking you. It may mean some real effort for him to climax. It could mean other forms of sexual activity. So be open to his openness; invite it by asking, "What would you *really* like to do?"

Some men from extremely repressed backgrounds, find an invitation like this daunting. It may be difficult for them even to imagine verbalizing this so freely. If he can not answer you, say, "That's OK. Just think about it, and maybe you can tell me later."

In this case, you are not prying something from him, and perhaps when he feels freer about sexuality he can answer you, or show you, later.

The art of seduction seeks to produce an atmosphere of intimacy, openness, and fun. You cannot always guarantee this will be happening, but it should be kept in mind. Often there is so much shame involved with sexual dysfunction that this intimacy, openness, and fun get lost. The important thing is to try to keep them there, and not get dragged down by what can be the half-hidden shadow of shame in the problem. As I said earlier in discussing problems versus "issues," problems can be faced and dealt with. As an "issue" that will not be openly faced, sexual dysfunction can continue to destroy the atmosphere of seduction.

WORH FOR YOU: Can you remember a situation where sexual dysfunction was experienced but not talked about? Many years ago, I had an alcoholic friend whose substance abuse problem led directly to sexual dysfunction, which only increased his alcohol problems. Since I was still in my twenties and he was almost two decades older, I felt unable to broach this with him; it eventually destroyed his life. If you have had such a situation, think about how bringing it up might have changed things and how, being more in control of the situation, it might be possible for you to be the agent of this change. (I say "might" because you are still dealing with a difficult situation, either your own dysfunction or someone else's; however, it is within the art of seduction to feel safer about bringing it up.)

WORH SPACE:

_____

_____

_____

_____

_____

_____

_____

_____

_____

42 Seduction and "Straight" Men

> "'I think also that you are beautiful,' said Birkin to
> Gerald, 'and that is enjoyable, too. One should
> enjoy what is given.'
> 'You think I am beautiful—how do you mean,
> physically?' asked Gerald, his eyes glistening."
> D. H. Lawrence, *Women in Love*

One thing becomes apparent in any discussion of seduction and "straight" men (I use quotes around "straight" because the term seems to get looser every day, but I won't use the quotes after this): straight men *are* seductive. At work, over conference tables, on the phone, at boys' nights out at bars, in sports—a huge amount of the way straight men interact with each other is *seduction*. The question is, how far will they go, and the answer is, sometimes very far. Often, this is in the realm of "Was I drunk last night!" But even more often, they get drunk in order to bring themselves to that wobbly, strange territory where they will do anything.

A lot of alcoholic gay men started out as straight, and because of their need to be drunk before they could have sex, ended up with a drinking problem. When the drinking backfires into problems of uncontrollable anger, rage, and hostility, violence results. So beware of the "Boy, was I drunk last night!" situation. It can easily swerve into the "Boy, was *I* beaten up this morning, because he couldn't take what happened when *he* got drunk last night."

This leads me into why straight men are so seductive, and why we are interested in them when they are (and sometimes when they are not).

Straight men are seductive because they want the attention of other men, and gay men are very good at giving men attention. We are sensitive, concerned, focused, buddyish, and fun. A lot of straight men are desperate for this kind of attention from another man, and they know that an almost guaranteed way to get it is by leading us on. They also like the turnaround of being the object of desire, since in most mainstream (i.e. conservative) communities and cultures women are still trained not to openly find men desirable.

Straight men know they can get this attention from a gay man, whom they may know is gay (or pretend not to know), and they know that the way to keep on getting this attention is by leading a gay friend into more and more intimate areas.

In my younger years I found this situation going on constantly from straight bosses, colleagues at work, men who were selling me insurance, men I traveled with, servicemen I met. It became more of a bother than a turn-on, because I knew exactly where it was coming from: a need for attention and not from sexual interest.

But it is easy to find yourself in this situation, and at a certain point, both you and your straight buddy may even find yourselves "committing to the ball."

The question is, why would you find straight men attractive? (Don't laugh. We do need to get through this question.)

First, straight men are off-limits, and ever since Eve took that bite out of the Forbidden Fruit, there's been nothing like what's off-limits to make even the most mundane apple seem desirable. If you feel that only gay guys feel this way, realize that huge amounts of straight porn deal with off-limits ladies, like nuns, female bosses, doctors, cops, college profs, and moms.

Also, there are a lot of attractive men out there who are straight, or tell you they are, and sometimes the fact that they are not "professionally queer" yet, makes them seem even more appealing.

I'm not sure if it's because they have a different, more direct energy or only seem to, but sometimes, and for some gay men, there is a difference in the quality of friendship they have with straight guys that can be intoxicating in itself. You feel that they really "get" you; that they are not just judging you on your surface attractiveness, your Kenneth Cole outfits, or if you're ordering the latest martini from Absolut. They're still drinking Bud, and happy with it.

Historically, when the "gay/straight" binary system of sexual categorization wasn't so set in stone, men whom society called "queer" were referred to as "fairies," and often, in various forms of feminine drag, they trolled the backstreets of big cities looking for "trade." "Trade" was straight men who liked to be serviced (sucked off), or who liked to anonymously fuck other men. So this straight/gay dynamic has been going on for a long time. The old joke was, "Yesterday's trade is tomorrow's competition." In other words, many straight men got "turned" gay because of their curiosity about gay sex, and after that went from barely willing "trade" status to very willing "fairy" or "queen" status.

It was true that this was how some men came to realize that they were really gay. They loved other men, wanted to find romance with them, and realized that this intensity of sexual interest was just not going to come with women. Still, there is that hazy, gray area, that used to be known in torrid paperback novels as "twilight sex," where the straight men suddenly appeared and the gay men were waiting, and a lot of men openly fantasized visiting that place, as a lot of men still do.

If you are in a situation of seduction with a straight man, it is usually one that both of you have placed yourselves in. The first rule is go slow. Rushing into this can be disastrous, even danger-ous. I know this from first-hand experience, having lived in a close to all male Air Force environment, where any unwanted gay intru-sion could mean death. You may not be in that extreme situation, but rushing in can result in crossed signals leading to confusion, anger, and hurt for both you and the man you're interested in. However, if you are still interested, understand that in these situations straight men are usually interested in one of two things:

1) A simple, uncomplicated sexual release. They may even go to rest stops, bathhouses, and other cruising areas to find this.

2) A sexual "friendship" with no romantic subtext. In other words, hotter "buddydom."

There is a third situation, in which the straight man comes out. But don't look forward to this too much, or invest any great hopes in it.

Push Comes to Shove

Now, the question is, if you're interested in sex with a straight man, and he is giving you signals that this "may" be possible, how do you move things further into that direction?

As in other aspects of the art of seduction, you need to show that you can be in control by revealing what you'd like. Don't ask him if he'd like to go to bed with you. This moves him into a territory of responsi-bility that he's working to get out of.

If he could tell you openly that he wanted to go to bed with you, it would place him outside of the "straight" focus or identity that he either wants or needs to stay in. So, at a certain point when you feel that you are both very comfortable with one another, say:

"I want to tell you that I find you attractive. I'd like to go to bed with you. I hope you want to. We won't do anything that you don't want to do." Then add, "Of course it's up to you."

This way, he's not making the decision, he's simply agreeing to it. Once in bed, you can actually let him lead, either by showing or telling you what he wants. A lot of gay men find this idea attractive, at least in the beginning. If this situation turns into an "affair," you may get bored with it after a while, and he may realize it and enlarge whatever sexual repertory he has.

A lot of straight men have the idea that everything's OK as long as they keep something out of the picture, which keeps them from being "queer." For instance, he may allow you to jerk him off, but refuse to let you to blow him. He might allow you to fuck him (after all, his wife can't do this), but he won't suck you. If he will suck, he won't kiss you. Or he will kiss you, but won't . . . anyway, you get the idea. There is someplace he will not go, and it's important for you to understand this, and not try to push him in that direction, or speed the way to it.

Also:

Don't try to get him drunk to get him into bed, a very volatile combination. Drugs, sex, and straight men together is asking for danger. Don't be drunk yourself, thinking that now he'll forgive your advances ("He was just drunk!"). You want to keep your wits with you.

And don't try to get him turned on with hetero porn, a cheap trick from the olden days, used by queens to get "trade" stiff and then serviced.

If you do, he will feel tricked, and not very happy about it.

Homosexual Panic, or "Queer Fear"

These two terms can be used almost interchangeably. Homosexual panic can come from an extremity of old-fashioned "queer fear," when suddenly a straight man realizes he has got in deeper than he expected, and feels trapped. Horrifying murders have resulted from homosexual panic, and in many areas of the country, until very recently, the term "homosexual panic" was a quick, very usable "Get Out Of Jail Free" card for crimes victimizing gay men. This is no longer the case, and even in the military "homosexual panic" is not the fail-safe defense it once was.

If you feel that he is going into this and a sudden rage is coming from him that you did not anticipate, try to get out of the situation as quickly and firmly as possible. Make sure that he understands that "nothing took place," that you are "sorry for any misunderstanding," and that you "did not mean any harm."

Don't try to call upon his "maturity" or "sophistication." But you can reinforce the feeling that he is a "good person and will understand that sometimes mistakes like this are made."

Then get out as fast as you can.

If you are at his place, leave. If he's at yours, try to get him out. Don't expect him to sleep this off and for things to get better in the morning. If you feel that he may become violent, you may want to ask for police protection, although this is a really tough call. Some cities have gay hotlines, and GLBT antiviolence groups. Look one up, even if it means calling long distance. A community relations officer within your police precinct can also be helpful. The problem is often that, unless a crime has already taken place, the police are not interested and/or cannot legally do anything.

Things Work Out

Sometimes, things can actually work out, as anyone who's ever been in an environment of "situational homosexuality" (prison, the military, to name two) can tell you. You can have a "straight boyfriend" who may have a girlfriend, or as black men say, is "on the downlow." How long you'll want to stay in this arrangement is up to you. However, for your own sanity, keep these ideas in mind:

Ask yourself what the real attraction of this situation is. How long will you be attracted to it, or to him?

Don't ask for things you can't get. If you get tired of being treated as merely "something for him to get off with," then find a way to get out of it. Don't ever think of blackmailing him to manipulate him, unless you really want trouble. But you can tell him that you've found a gay friend who can offer you what he can't, and remind him that he does have other people who are "very important" to him— such as a wife, girlfriend, or other straight friends.

Don't cut things off without an explanation. If you do, he may start stalking you, and this can become a very *bad* scene. After all, you've given him something that even a girlfriend or a wife can't: emotional and physical attention from a man. Many straight men are starved for this. In our homophobic, queer-paranoid society, for two straight men to have any kind of nourishing closeness without sexual undertones has become rare. So they are often on the prowl for it, whether or not they can admit it.

WORK FOR YOU: Think of straight men you've been attracted to. Were you in a situation to work on that attraction? Do you think you would be, now that I've brought up the subject and given it the context I have? Some gay men focus on straight men; they like the ambiguity, suspense, and even danger of the situation. Have you ever known any men like this? In many other countries and areas, such as the Middle East, where our idea of romantic gayness has barely surfaced, going after heterosexual men and having them come after you is almost the rule. Many Western gay men find this exciting. What would you think of it?

WORK SPACE:
Your thoughts—

_____

_____

_____

_____

_____

_____

_____

_____

_____

_____

43 Seduction and Married Men

"It would degrade me to marry Heathcliff now; so he shall never know how I love him: and that is not because he's handsome, Nelly, but because he's more myself than I am. Whatever our souls are made of, his and mine are the same; and Linton's is as different as a moonbeam from lightning, or frost from fire."

Emily Brontë, *Wuthering Heights*

After writing a chapter on "Monogamy and Seduction," including this chapter, its complete opposite, is asking for trouble, especially now when so many gay men are romantically looking for their One-and-Only. So this is another controversy-loaded chapter, but one I felt that, realistically, should be included here, although it may bother or even infuriate some readers. We are now living in a time of gay marriage, and the old idea of the "open gay relationship" seems antiquated to some people and even fake to others. What kind of "open" relationship could also be faithful, truthful, and trusting? Some men might answer, "The one I have!" But when so much is being invested in legalizing gay marriages, with attachments of property, homes, and kids, the idea of one member of such a relationship seeking sex or intimacy elsewhere seems particularly obnoxious or hurtful.

(And I can say that straying within a marriage can cause real pain to the other partner, although maybe not as much pain as actually breaking up the marriage.)

But I want this book to be realistic as well as idealistic.

Marriage has often been called "the world's loneliest arrangement," when the sparkle, newness, and romance of something has worn off and one of the partners—or both—finds himself living with a stranger he can barely talk to. Thousands of books, plays, movies, and TV series have been written about married men and why they stray, but the truth is that you can easily find yourself in a seductive situation with one of them.

Usually when this happens they are so fast to bite (in a friendly manner) at any suggestion of attention, sex, or affection, that it might shock you. Often, whether they'll admit it or not, they are looking for you as much as you may be at some point (at a party, a bar, or in a casual situation) looking *at* them.

One gay man I knew who was married for a long time before he came out and left his marriage told me: "Married men can usually spot one another. We have a different look than other gay men. It's more concerned, anxious, and worried. We have kids to worry about, and money and time factors. So often gay married men look for other married men who understand this." Two married men who are gay will have even more time-scheduling problems to deal with, so the fact that you are unattached may really appeal to an attached man looking for attention elsewhere.

But why should you, as a single gay man, be interested in a married man, either gay or primarily straight, or bisexual?

First, let's deal with attraction, how you deal with that, and whether his circumstances and yours have enough in common to make this work. If you are attracted to him and know he's married, you may simply ignore the attraction—and him—even though at some point he may show up again, and you may feel the attraction again. If he is curious about you and you are curious about him, then the circumstances may be right for something to happen. He may also be in a more "open" relationship, or one that has reached the point (especially true for gay men in gay relationships) where something can happen with you. And, because he's already in a relationship, he may seem more mature and responsible than single guys on the prowl whose main concern is their abs, biceps, and Calvin Klein jeans.

Second, you may like the fact that he has kids, thus giving you some access to a family, whether that access is open or not. Also, the "not professionally queer" aspect of many married men can be attractive and intriguing. Here's a guy who's had some real experience and on-the-job training in relationships. He's already had one going for a while. So he may be good at dealing with your "issues," rather than someone who's never been in any relationship and finds dealing with someone else's problems and limitations "so over that," even before it's started.

Third (and this can be very important to you), this kind of *limited* relationship may give you time to be yourself, by yourself. A lot of men feel that any relationship has got to be either "all or nothing," whether it's a hot one-night-stand or the total "love of my life" thing. Their demands are very high, and they often clang and bang their way through a series of attractions and connections before becoming very burned out from all of them.

After going through enough of these extremely demanding situations (even if the demands come from them), they may realize that having some time for themselves, away from him, can be, well, *wonderful*.

Although a lot of people may be judgmental about any relationship with a married man (or, if you are a married man reading this, they may be telling you exactly what you should be thinking), if you find yourself in this situation, it is possible to understand that having a relationship with a man who's already married can work—within the parameters of your own life and the other man's marriage.

Human beings have been doing it for thousands of years. There have actually been some famous "arrangements" in this regard, like Katharine Hepburn's long-running love affair with married Spencer Tracey, or the lesbian Vita Sackville-West's marriage to the gay Harold Nicholson, which produced two sons and myriad outside affairs for each of them, the most famous being Vita's affair with Virginia Woolf. (And I won't even go here into any of the Kennedys, or Bill Clinton: let's let sleeping dogs lie—mostly to their wives.)

Kate Hepburn was once asked if she would have married Tracy if he'd been available? She answered with a flat "No." She wanted her independence, and he understood this.

Some men hate the "home wrecker" role they feel they're in. But the truth is, the "other man" is often the one keeping the marriage going. Without his acceptance of the married man's status, the marriage might have fallen apart years ago, although this in itself can add to the trickiness of the situation. Depending upon your attraction and involvement, and his willingness to bend to the needs of two different people (you and his wife), it is possible for this arrangement to continue.

So if you are the involved with a married man, here are some ideas to keep in mind.

His time may be more pressured than yours. But your time, and his respect for it, is important. If he has to break a date with you, he should not be casual about it, with a "that's-the-way-things-go" attitude. It should not be that hard for him to be considerate and give you notice that he can't make it. Unless this is really only a casual, quicky affair, he should take your disappointment seriously.

You might like the "on the side" nature of this arrangement, but at a certain point get tired of it. Let him know, if and/when this happens. Don't just drop him because he can't offer you what he doesn't really have to offer: complete access to him. Treat each other with respect. If you feel that the respect is only coming from you, let him know it.

Closets (full of secrets) give people at least an idea of protection. He's trying to protect his marriage and himself. So protect yourself, too. You might want to date other men, and not lock yourself into a situation that can end quickly.

On the other hand, secrets and secretive relationships can add a certain glamour, intimacy, and closeness to what happens between the two of you that many more open arrangements may not have. This is often part of the initial heat involved in affairs with married men. After all, when he is with you, he really does belong to you in this intimate, closed region between the two of you. Against all odds, you still have him all to yourself.

This is in contrast with your regular daily life and his, when you deal with sixteen of your best friends, coworkers, and gym buddies, and he has his various minions, etc. all of whom may be itching to know what's going on and feel they have a right to mull over it, like the catty girlfriends in *The Women* dying to know the dirt and come crashing in where they have no real business.

You may feel lonely with this secret, but there can also be a lot of vitality in it. This is often what keeps clandestine affairs going, so much so that when they cease to be secret a lot of the heat and sparkle goes out of them, too.

If you are the married man and you've done this before (as lots of married men have), then arrange some real time when the two of you can be together, like a weekend trip. This is a very volatile situation, but your spouse may already have an idea that something is going on. The question is, how far do the three of you want to go with this, and how open can you be about it?

Millions of gay men are still married to women. Their wives understood years ago that in order to keep their marriages going they have to allow things they never expected at the altar. Being more open about what is happening may actually be good for her, too. And you may feel that the one thing neither of you want to do is to break up the marriage, especially if kids are involved.

Safe sex here is very important. A lot of married men have the illusion that they "cannot get HIV" because they're married. So the truth is, neither of you should take foolish chances.

Unlike with straight single men, married men, whether they are married to a man or to a woman, usually have more of an idea what they actually want. They have been around the block, at least as far as seductions are concerned. If he's married and seeks you out and also knows you're gay, there is a good chance that sex with you is somewhere in the back of his mind.

It may be really far back, and he may not want to admit it, but it's there. If this is something you want, and you are going into it with your eyes open, don't be afraid to lay your cards on the table.

A good approach is simply:

"I'd like to know what you have in mind. Tell me. I'd like to go to bed with you, and want to know if you're interested."

He may act coy about this, since coyness may be a behavior that he learned years ago is safe. If you feel that he's not being coy but simply wants to play games with you, you may decide not to pursue this. However, realize that often beneath his coyness and shyness may lie a real desire to be sexual with you.

Including this chapter on married men and seduction will probably get me into trouble in some circles (although some people may find the whole book troublesome: I hope you're not one of them). It is opening up a large can of worms. However, seduction is based on your own feeling of security, power, and self-knowledge. So not talking about seduction and marriage would constitute a worse lie than *any* he is telling his wife, or husband.

WORH FOR YOU: What are your feelings about marriage? Would they ever include having an affair? If you are married and had an affair, would the marriage be over?

WORH SPACE:
Your feeling—

_____

_____

_____

_____

_____

_____

_____

_____

_____

CHAPTER 44 Seduction and Threesomes

One of the nicer things about many long-term gay relationships is that if a third man gets involved, it can become a threesome. Traditionally, many gay men in couple relationships have valued threesomes, or a *ménage à trois* as the French call them. But now in our age of Neo-Victorian, idealized gay monogamy, where David Sedaris has become one of the chief public voices for a Gap-khaki generation of frustrated young gay men, the threesome has taken on a bad rep. It's like bringing the cynically-named gay three D's of the 1960s and 1970s ("Drugs, Dick, and Disco!") into a highly regulated "domestic partnership" environment that loves to loathe them.

This is sad, because for many unattached men, threesomes can be powerfully hot, exciting, and emotionally more satisfying than eons of one-night stands, done singly, with guys who can't see beyond their noses. Many of these pairs of men have already seen way beyond their own noses: they *are* in a relationship. They know what it's like to be romantically involved with someone else, and often they are good at making the first move or knowing the signals when that move has been made toward them.

In a more open relationship, threesomes begin when one member of the couple finds you in a bar or a party situation; you have a one-nighter, and then he introduces you to his partner. What threesomes need (and spark) is a feeling of spontaneity in sex. You are not going to meet these two guys and negotiate for the next six weeks of dating whether or not to go to bed. Usually the two men will want to do this very fast.

You now have two suitors instead of one. You may feel pressured about this, but the reason why the French call the third person in a three-some "Lucky Pierre" is that he can be the person who decides what is going to happen, who'll do what to whom, and who will receive most of the attention.

This is the way it *should* happen, but not all couples are gifted in the art of seduction (and have been blessed by its more famous Muses—

Helen of Troy, Zsa Zsa Gabor, Cary Grant, Kathy Griffith, to name a few). You may feel pressured and used. But the truth is, you don't have to feel like their little fuckbunny for the night, unless you *really* want to.

The easiest way to prevent this is by being honest and asking some questions:

"What are you guys into? What do you really want?"

And then: "Let me tell you what I'm really interested in."

If you feel that this is being met with resistance, then just consider, as in any other seductive situation, that this may not work.

Tell them honestly: "I'm sorry. This is not something I feel that I want to do."

It does not take a lot of brains for you to understand that if you feel in the least bit uncomfortable with what's going on, to get the hell out. For your own safety and happiness, don't end up with two guys who can overpower you. Male rape is real, and a threesome can end up that way. Know what you're getting into, and tell them exactly how you feel about it.

"I'm not sure that I know either of you that well."

"I'm sorry, I don't feel safe about this."

"This is something that I'd really like to do, but I want to make it plain that I need to have my own boundaries respected."

Once you get all of your cards on the table, and feel safe (an extremely important consideration, let me repeat), threesomes can be deliciously enjoyable. As in any married situation, however, there are usually time limitations, although some threesomes have gone on for years. One of the most famous was the high-talent threesome that entailed the writer Glenway Wescott, his lover the curator Monroe Wheeler, and the younger, famous photographer George Platt Lynes. Threesomes were the only way Wescott could really be excited sexually. This threesome lasted for about eight years, and the members continued as friends and lovers in various permutations for decades.

If you are looking for a threesome and you become aware that the man you're seducing has a partner, then sometime in the seduction process tell him, "I'd like to meet your lover. I think that would be nice. Do you think he'd be interested in meeting me?"

Sometimes the man you're with may himself not be interested in pursuing this. But sometimes he may be clumsily trying to hint at it (and is turning all sparkles inside at the thought of it). That you are taking control of this situation means he won't have to go through a lot of choreography to get you (and his partner) into bed.

If you have been approached by a couple, it's easiest when you are attracted to both men. The downside is when two men come on to you, and you only want one of them. This is a sticky situation. How do you turn the offered threesome into a twosome with one of them, without the third man feeling hurt, rejected, or threatened?

The thing to do is not simply to concentrate on the man you're attracted to, but to make his partner feel that you also have some warm feelings toward him. After the three of you have had sex, make it clear to the man you're attracted to that he is the one you're interested in, but you'll understand if he does not want to continue seeing you alone.

As you can see, situations involving straight men, married men, and threesomes can be complicated. They have their pros and cons. The most obvious pro is your attraction to the man involved and how much you feel the need to respond to that attraction. Included in this equation should also be some attention to the person you don't see: If you are involved with a married man, think about what his wife or husband may be going through, and if your presence is working to maintain their relationship or destroying it. These situations require you to be an adult. Sometimes the attraction fades once you realize what the odds for success are, especially if success in your book is that you will ride off in the sunset together, set up housekeeping, and live happily ever after.

If success means working on a mutual attraction, making your intentions known to him, acting on those intentions, and negotiating sexual situations that please you both (or them), and also being mindful of not hurting other people, then you've been *very* successful. Your feelings for yourself as a desirable person have been enlarged, recognized, deeply felt. And this certainly goes for a three-some, when they work at their best.

WORK FOR YOU: Think about what you feel might be a great fantasy threesome, and I don't mean one involving you, Michael Lucas, and Jeff Stryyker. I mean one with two friends who are either together or who might be together with you. Is this something you never imagined before? Can you allow yourself to enter into it as a fantasy? If this kind of experience does come along, at least you'll have had the experience first in your head. The next time you are with a married gay friend, ask him if he's ever been in a threesome, and how he felt about it. He may look at you strangely, but at least you can talk with him about something that too many people cover up.

WORK SPACE:

Your idea of a great threesome—

_____

_____

_____

_____

_____

_____

_____

_____

_____

_____

45 Being Seduced by Seduction

"Be seduced by the role."
Albert Collum, master teacher of Shakespeare

"I have made the most out of the situation in
which I have placed myself."
Archie Leach (a.k.a. Cary Grant)

It is easy to be seduced by seduction, to find your own mastery of this art
leading you into places you never thought you could go, some of which
are wonderful and others possibly . . . well, much less wonderful. As
with magic, psychology, or any other form of manipulating humans, their
perceptions, and reactions, seduction has to be handled responsibly, both
for your sake and the sake of others. One of the things I learned as a seductive child, and then a seductive adult, was the limits of seduction and
how startling they can be. Just when you think you can get it all, you find
out you can't. You can be seduced by seduction, wading into waters you
cannot swim in, falling in love with your own power to seduce, with the
sheer delight of it happening.

Much of our TV mythology is based on the very idea: that the right
seductive behavior and its subsequent events lead to ultimate happiness
and success. So many "reality" programs have this built in as a premise.
The most seductive girl will get the ultimate bachelor (or vice versa for
the perfect bachelorette). You can use seduction at work and rise to the
top without talent (OK, that does work, *sometimes*). You can seduce
yourself (and him) into long-lasting happiness.

None of this is necessarily true, yet I can't say that it is one hundred
percent *un*true. There are no guarantees, except to say that your judg-
ment and maturity can lead you, through the avenues of seduction, to
important and fulfilling relationships.

What seduction *can* do is take you out of the rut so many people feel
trapped in, the imprisonment of isolation, insecurity, and powerless-
ness. As the seducer, you are taking on the mantle of your own power
and security. You are also giving attention to many men who, today,

may not get it in any other form. This in itself is a beautiful thing, and nothing to sniff at.

So before you go off and start practicing this art in social/sexual situations, realize that while part of seduction is seducing yourself— recognizing this best, desirable, interesting aspect of you—a very important part is realizing its limitations. Many horses don't want to be led to any kind of water. Seducing a man does not make him love you, but allowing him to see your lovable qualities can be very helpful. Falling head over heels with every man you seduce is not using your brain. And always remember: using your brain is perhaps the important part of what makes seduction work.

46 The Uses and Boundaries of Seduction

"Falling in love with love / is falling for make
believe."
Lorenz Hart, "Falling in Love with Love"

Seduction has many uses, and we see them all the time. We are constantly being seduced by politicians, car salesmen, real estate agents, hair stylists and anyone else whose livelihood depends upon the whims and goodwill of the public. You can take much of this more public form of seduction with a very large grain of salt—or plain common sense.

But the seduction I've dealt with in this book is different. It can take you from being alone, feeling like a passive participant in what seems like pure chance, to the active player in the rites of sex and courtship, and being with the right "him."

But it cannot take you a lot further unless you mature with it.

Seduction is not an end run around maturity. I certainly learned this growing up in the South, where seduction was so common, such a normal part of interactions that it was often not easy to see it in a more real context. After years of socializing and training, men and women learned to show an amazing amount of personal, flattering attention to just about everyone. As a small child I adored this, loved having adults coming down to my level to look me straight in the eye and tell me how handsome I was, how clever, how special, how bright. I also learned how important it was to compliment them in return, smile in just right way, and not ignore someone when being spoken to.

As a young adult returning home, I saw that these behaviors were still in practice, but after years of living in competitive New York, it was easy to misinterpret them. Not every man down South who smiled at you and looked you in the eye was interested in you sexually. It was simply the habit of seduction, and often, behind it, homophobia was cruising shark-like under the surface, engaged in its own struggle with suppressed homosexual feelings. These situations and the signals around them have, even when read correctly, caused terrible harm to many gay men.

Therefore, while being seduced by seduction is easy, knowing its limitations are extremely important. Knowing, for instance, that you cannot (and should not) use the same techniques over and over just for the thrill of it. Men will figure out that this is your routine, and at a certain point avoid you. Seduction without growth is a blind alley, and I hope you don't end up in it.

As a means of coming out of your own isolation, of knowing how to make other men comfortable with you, and of how to direct intimate relationships so that they overcome some of the ice and obstacles around them, seduction is a wonderful tool. And I hope that you will use it with wisdom and care.

Finally, here are some recaps to remember:

Seduction is taking responsibility for your own actions. It is realizing that you are secure enough and capable of initiating interest in someone. It is knowing that you can come out of yourself enough to recognize the attractiveness of other guys.

You need to have all of your senses open while doing this. Your sense of yourself and of him. Don't attempt this while you are drunk, drugged, tired, or desperate enough to get yourself into trouble.

Realize that sometimes things just don't work out. The truth is that people often reject others because they cannot even *imagine* acceptance. They have been programmed as part of our culture of rejection to put rigid boundaries around themselves. They would reject anyone, not simply you.

Don't play games with people. Realize that their feelings are as important as your own, and you are an adult now. Men who use seduction as a game, trying to chalk up conquests that are easily erased in their heads, are only asking for defeat. A lot of men reading this book will say, "Why don't you have a scoring system for success? Let's make seduction into a parlor game, or a pastime."

Seduction is not a game. We're not deaing with *Les Liaisons Dangereuses* (the novel that was the basis for a successful play and movie, *Dangerous Liaisons*). We're dealing with your handling a potentially potent and sensitive situation, so that meeting and dealing with other men in a natural manner can work in the normal course of your life.

Invite, and expect, some sense of adventure in your life. Sex, love, and art all have in common a feeling that some wonderful element of revelation and even happiness is hidden within. To find it, you may have to scrape off a lot of fear and jadedness either in yourself or others, but when you do, it will make reading this book very worthwhile.

Some Final Thoughts

Seduction is part of the dance of life. The fact that I expressed it here as an art form makes it approachable, teachable, and understandable, as any art form can be. It can also be seen through its laughing spontaneity, its loving goodness, and its mindfulness. You can learn to be mindful of another person, and of yourself, and even of yourself as another person, one you are approaching with love and forgiveness.

In the great run of the world, seduction is what God does to us when this great Force or Thing or Being invites us to sit in calm, peace, and acceptance, and to *know*. To finally, wondrously *know*.

CODA
More Important Tools You Can Use in the Manly Art of Seduction

Although I've ended many of the preceding chapters with a section called "WORK FOR YOU," with exercises to help you hone your own gifts in the manly art of seduction, in the next sections I want to give you more advanced mental tools to help you become the artful seducer you want to be.

Basically, this is to make you understand that seduction is really about mindfulness, something that Zen masters have been practicing for thousands of years. It is about using your own intelligence in situations where fear, shame, and other inhibiting factors are often at work to keep you in a passive, dumb, and unsatisfied place of aloneness and emptiness.

Seduction is about getting out of those terrible pits of aloneness and emptiness. It is about becoming active, resourceful, and mindful.

Those Unbidden Gifts Again

I want you to think about some gift that was given to you in the past, something that carried some real importance to you. It can be a toy, a personal object, or even a moment to which you felt particularly attached. Now, "valorize" this gift. Mentally, increase its value. Picture it in a wonderful box, shining, gleaming with light coming from it. Think of it as a magic charm you are holding close to you. Next, imagine being in a room with thirty or forty men who are basically strangers, not personal friends. It can be a bar you go to, or a meeting if you are a member of an organization. If you'd like, you can do this the next time you are actually in such a room with a number of real men you might want to meet on a more intimate level.

Now pick out seven men, and smile. Imagine giving this "charm" to them. They have just received this wonderful gift from you with its own personal meaning. Imagine the warmth they will feel getting this gift.

Now I want you to think of another gift. Again it's something from your past, something you might have a hard time parting with. But you want to give it to a very special person.

Think of it as a very valuable thing in its new box, straight from Fifth Avenue. Maybe from Tiffany's or someplace you're sure will make this gift seem even more elegant and special. You're not going to give it to seven guys this time. This is a more personal gift. It's only going to three men.

Pick out these three guys—you might even have had your eyes on them before, and imagine giving this unbidden gift to them. They had no idea what was coming, but you're offering them something that means a lot to you, and feel that they will accept it in the spirit that you are offering it.

Now, finally, we're going to come to the last gift. And I'm sure you know this is the really *great* one. I want you to think of this gift as being truly an item representing love, tenderness, and in truth, real "emotional currency." That is, it represents some genuine feelings and resources from you. No matter what the gift is, it did not come cheap. It came through your own experiences, life story, and life struggle. It represents your own overcoming shyness, doubt, and fear. You're going to put it in its own very special box that shows you are conscious of its value. Just imagine this, and imagine that this is *the* unbidden gift that you want to give to a very special person. Someone waiting in an empty place in your heart. Can you can see this?

Good.

Now I want you to give this gift that comes from your own deep heart to *every* man in the room. And later, when you look at these men, realize that they all have this one, last, special gift. And it came from you.

Do this exercise a few times and then see how it affects your going into a room full of strangers. That each man is a potential recipient of a gift from you adds a lot of interest and excitement to any group of men. The only question left is how will you give them this gift, and how will they receive it. Because their reception is very telling, and, as in the case of all unbidden gifts, it will show you a lot about them. But what is even more important is that you have had the imagination and courage to offer it.

Particularity

Particularity is one of the most difficult concepts to grasp, because it is so outside our culture of mass consumerism and mass consumerism is based on a rejection of the idea of particularity. Every McDonald's wants to show you that every single Big Mac it sells, no matter where it sells it, is identical to every other Big Mac. When you shop at one Target you'll find there what every other Target carries. Likewise, in much of the working world employers like to show that no one is indispensable. Everyone can be replaced by someone else who is basically like them.

None of this takes into account the deepest aspects of our selves, which are so individual, so intrinsic to our own stories and experiences— so *particular.*

Our deepest emotional satisfaction is dependent on understanding our own particularity and how it operates. Each of us is an individual, someone aside from a "type," beyond any faulty first impression others may get based on either your defensiveness or his own. We now live with this huge idea of "What You See Is What You Get." or "Image is everything," and I must admit that I am as taken with a great exterior package as anyone. But I have also learned that it is possible to relax enough to invite the particularity of other men.

That is, to see them as unique, interesting, exciting, and even wonderful.

Here are some reasons why men often fail to open themselves up to the *particularity* of other guys.

They are so scared of how they are perceived by other men that they can't really look at them to find out.

They have such a set image in their mind of who their "type" is that they cannot open themselves up to different kinds of men, and see that there is an excitement inside men as well as outside them.

They expect so much out of themselves that they cannot relax even when alone, so it's out of the question that they can relax enough with other men to see them differently.

Here is an exercise in relaxing enough to feel the particularity of other men, to be able to particularize them and see something more in them than just another guy who looks like just another "type."

Before you go out into social/sexual situations, relax yourself. Don't think about what can happen or what will not happen. If you're going out with friends, don't let their expectations or snide remarks make you feel bad about yourself. ("He's such a dog, that's all he can get." "No one would ever look at him for his body." "With a face like that, what does he expect?")

Remember that remarks like this are reflections of your friends' own insecurities. Understand that you can become secure enough in yourself, enjoying your own feelings enough, that you don't have to be bothered by them.

When you go out into your normal course of events and see other men, ask yourself questions about them.

I wonder what his life is like?

Where does he come from?

What's inside his mind right now? What's he thinking about?

Instead of nervously dismissing guys, bring them closer to you. Imagine them opening themselves up to you, giving you something that many people normally would not see, no matter how they appear on the outside. Learn to repeat this exercise often, asking yourself questions about men even before you meet them. Then you will be more prepared for what they have to say once you do talk.

I have found that the sexiest men are the ones who have the most interesting stories. Luckily, I've been able to share an amazing number of these stories, sexually and otherwise.

I hope that this book will enable you to share many of these particular stories, and to add some of your own. Please feel free to get back to me with your stories, adventures, and ideas. This book is meant to be an adventure itself, a workbook, and an opening to your own deeper, seductive, and beautiful self.

the end

Perry Brass

Originally from Savannah, Georgia, Perry Brass grew up in the 1950s and 1960s, equal parts Southern, Jewish, economically impoverished, and very much *gay*. To escape the South's violent homophobia, he hitchhiked at seventeen from Savannah to San Francisco—an adventure, he recalls, that was "like Mark Twain with drag queens." He has published fifteen books and been a finalist six times for Lambda Literary Awards in poetry, gay science fiction and fantasy, and spirituality and religion. His novels *Warlock* and *Carnal Sacraments* both received "Ippy" Awards from *Independent Press Magazine* as Best Gay and Lesbian Book. *Carnal Sacraments* was also a finalist for a Best Book of the Year Award from *ForeWord* magazine.

He has been involved in the gay movement since 1969, when he co-edited *Come Out!*, the world's first gay liberation newspaper. In 1972, with two friends he started the Gay Men's Health Project Clinic, the first clinic for gay men on the East Coast, still surviving as New York's Callen-Lorde Community Health Center. In 1984, his play *Night Chills*, one of the first plays to deal with the AIDS crisis, won a Jane Chambers International Gay Playwriting Award. Brass's numerous collaborations with composers include the poetry for "All the Way Through Evening," a five-song cycle set by the late Chris DeBlasio; "The Angel Voices of Men" set by Ricky Ian Gordon, commissioned by the Dick Cable Fund for the New York City Gay Men's Chorus, which featured it on its *Gay Century Songbook* CD; "Three Brass Songs" set by Fred Hersch; "Five 'Russian' Lyrics," set by Christopher Berg, commissioned by Positive Music; and "Waltzes for Men," also commissioned by the DCF for the NYC Gay Men's Chorus, set by Craig Carnahan. His latest musical collaboration,"The Restless Yearning Towards My Self," set by opera composer Paula Kimper, was commissioned by Downtown Music.

Perry Brass is an accomplished reader and authority on gender subjects, gay relationships, and the history and literature of the movement towards glbt equality. He has taught numerous workshops and classes in writing and publishing fiction, and on the hidden roots of gay culture. He lives in the Riverdale section of "da Bronx," but can cross bridges to other parts of America without a passport.

Other Books by Perry Brass

SEX-CHARGE

". . . poetry at its highest voltage . . ."

Marv. Shaw in *Bay Area Reporter*.

Sex-charge. 76 pages. $6.95. With male photos by Joe Ziolkowski.
ISBN 0-9627123-0-2

MIRAGE

ELECTRIFYING SCIENCE FICTION

A gay science fiction classic! An original "coming out" and coming-of-age saga, set in a distant place where gay sexuality and romance is a norm, but with a life-or-death price on it. On the tribal planet Ki, two men have been promised to each other for a lifetime. But a savage attack and a blood-chilling murder break this promise and force them to seek another world, where imbalance and lies form Reality. This is the planet known as Earth, a world they will use and escape. Finalist, 1991 Lambda Literary Award for Gay Men's Science Fiction/Fantasy. This classic work of gay science fiction fantasy is now available in its new Tenth Anniversary Edition.

"Intelligent and intriguing." Bob Satuloff in *The New York Native*.

Mirage, Tenth Anniversary Edition. 230 pages. $12.95.
ISBN 1-892149-02-8

CIRCLES

THE AMAZING SEQUEL TO *MIRAGE*

"The world Brass has created with *Mirage* and its sequel rivals, in complexity and wonder, such greats as C. S. Lewis and Ursula LeGuin." *Mandate Magazine*, New York.

Circles. 224 pages. $11.95.
ISBN 0-9627123-3-7

OUT THERE

STORIES OF PRIVATE DESIRES. HORROR. AND THE AFTERLIFE.
". . . we have come to associate [horror] with slick and trashy chiller-thrillers. Perry Brass is neither. He writes very well in an elegant and easy prose that carries the reader forward pleasurably. I found this selection to be excellent." The **Gay Review**, Canada.
Out There. 196 pages. $10.95.
ISBN 0-9627123-4-5

ALBERT

or THE BOOK OF MAN
Third in the *Mirage* trilogy. In 2025 the White Christian Party has taken over America. Albert, son of Enkidu and Greeland, must find the male Earth mate who will claim his heart and allow him to return to leadership on Ki. "Brass gives us a book where lesser writers would have only a premise." *Men's Style,* New York.
"If you take away the plot, it has political underpinnings that are chillingly true. Brass has a genius for the future." *Science Fiction Galaxies*, Columbus, OH. "Erotic suspense and action . . . a pleasurable read." *Screaming Hyena Review*, Melbourne, Australia.
Albert. 210 pages. $11.95.
ISBN 0-9627123-5-3

Works

AND OTHER "SMOKY GEORGE" STORIES, EXPANDED EDITION
"Classic Brass," these stories—many set in the long-gone seventies, when, as the author says, "Gay men cruised more and networked less"—have recharged gay erotica. This Expanded Edition contains a selection of Brass's steamy poems, as well as his essay "Maybe We Should Keep the 'Porn' in Pornography."
Works. 184 pages. $9.95.
ISBN 0-9627123-6-1

THE HARVEST

A "SCIENCE/POLITICO" NOVEL

From today's headlines predicting human cloning comes the emergence of "vaccos"—living "corporate cadavers"—raised to be sources of human organ and tissue transplants. One exceptional vacco will escape. His survival will depend upon Chris Turner, a sexual renegade who will love him and kill to keep him alive.

"One of the Ten Best Books of 1997," *Lavender Magazine*, Minneapolis. "In George Nader's *Chrome*, the hero dared to fall in love with a robot. In *The Harvest*—*a vastly superior novel*, Chris Turner falls in love with a vacco, Hart256043." Jesse Monteagudo, *The Weekly News*, Miami, Florida.

Finalist, 1997 Lambda Literary Award, Gay and Lesbian Science Fiction.

The Harvest. 216 pages. $11.95.
ISBN 0-9627123-7-X

THE LOVER OF MY SOUL

A SEARCH FOR ECSTASY AND WISDOM

Brass's first book of poetry since *Sex-charge* is worth the wait. Flagrantly erotic and just plain flagrant—with poems like "I Shoot the Sonovabitch Who Fires Me," "Sucking Dick Instead of Kissing," and the notorious "MTV Ab(*solutely*) Vac(*uous*) Awards, *The Lover of My Soul* again proves Brass's feeling that poetry must tell, astonish, and delight.

"An amazingly powerful book of poetry and prose," **The Loving Brotherhood**, Plainfield, NJ.

The Lover of My Soul. 100 pages. $8.95.
ISBN 0-9627123-8-8

How to survive your *own* gay life

AN ADULT GUIDE TO LOVE, SEX, AND RELATIONSHIPS
The book for adult gay men. About sex and love, and coming out of repression; about surviving homophobic violence; about your place in a community, a relationship, and a culture. About the important psychic "gay work" and the gay tribe. About dealing with conflicts and crises, personal, professional, and financial. And, finally, about being more alive, happier, and stronger.

"This book packs a wallop of wisdom!" **Morris Kight, founder, Los Angeles Gay & Lesbian Services Center.** Finalist, 1999 Lambda Literary Award in Gay and Lesbian Religion and Spirituality.

How to Survive Your Own Gay Life. 224 pages. $11.95.
ISBN 0-9627123-9-6

ANGEL LUST

AN EROTIC NOVEL OF TIME TRAVEL
Tommy Angelo and Bert Knight are in a long-term relationship. *Very* long—close to a millennium. Tommy and Bert are angels, but different. No wings. Sexually free. Tommy was once Thomas Jebson, a teen serf in the violent England of William the Conqueror. One evening he met a handsome knight who promised to love him for all time. Their story introduces us to gay forest men, robber barons, castles, and deep woodlands. Also, to a modern sexual underground where "gay" and "straight" mean little. To Brooklyn factory men. Street machos. New York real estate sharks. And the kind of lush erotic encounters for which Perry Brass is famous. Finalist, 2000 Lambda Literary Award, Gay and Lesbian Science Fiction.

"Brass's ability to go from seedy gay bars in New York to 11th century castles is a testament to his skill as a writer." *Gay & Lesbian Review.*

Angel Lust. 224 pages. $12.95.
ISBN 1-892149-00-1

Warlock

A NOVEL OF POSSESSION

Allen Barrow, a shy bank clerk, dresses out of discount stores and has a small penis that embarrasses him. One night at a bathhouse he meets Destry Powars—commanding, vulgar, seductive, successful—who pulls Allen into his orbit and won't let go. Destry lives in a closed moneyed world that Allen can only glimpse through the pages of tabloids. From generations of drifters, Powars has been chosen to learn a secret language based on force, deception, and nerve. But *who* chose him—and what does he really want from Allen? What *are* Mr. Powars's dark powers? These are the mysteries that Allen will uncover in *Warlock*, a novel that is as paralyzing in its suspense as it is voluptuously erotic.

Warlock. 226 pages. $12.95.
ISBN 1-892149-03-6

the Substance of God

A SPIRITUAL THRILLER

What would you do with the Substance of God, a self-regenerating material originating from Creation? The Substance can bring the dead back to life, but has a "mind" of its own. Dr. Leonard Miller, a gay bio-researcher secretly addicted to "kinky" sex, learned this after he was found mysteriously murdered in his laboratory while working alone on the Substance. Once brought back to life, Miller must find out who infiltrated his lab to kill him, how long will he have to live—and, *exactly*, where does life end and any Hereafter begin?

Miller's story takes him from the underground sex scenes of New York to the all-male baths of Istanbul. It will deal with the longing for God in a techno-driven world; with the persistent attractions of religious fundamentalism; and with the fundamentals of "outsider" sexuality as both spiritual ritual and cosmic release. And Miller, the unbelieving scientist, will be driven himself to ask one more question: Is our often-censored urge toward sex and our great, undeniable urge toward a union with God . . . the *same* urge?

"Perry Brass has added to the annals of gay lit." **Book Marks**.

The Substance of God. 232 pages. $13.95.
ISBN: 1-892149-04-4

CARNAL SACRAMENTS

A Historical Novel of the Future

In the last quarter of the 21st century, Jeffrey Cooper has made a Faustian pact with the global economic system running the world. No matter what age he is, the system will secretly keep him young and razor-sharp, as long as he can stay on top of his job and keep profits high. But Cooper has a problem: work stress and the congested, hyper-competitive life around him is killing him. Can he keep his stress level a secret from the system itself, his coworkers, and even his own seductive "daddyish" German therapist who has told him that when all else fails there are "angels" in the world who can save him, and often we don't know who they are?

One of them, in the most violent form, will appear in Jeffrey's life. At first, he seems to be the Devil himself, offering every kind of excitement, even offering Jeffrey back his lost soul. Will this younger, extremely mysterious and attractive man end up killing Jeffrey or saving him? *Carnal Sacraments* is a parable of our time and the future, of the all-swallowing global economy, of an emerging international business culture based on war, and of the real keys to religious experience and personal salvation.

"Layered with philosophical elements, fascinating descriptions, and a clear focus on character overall, Brass's latest work is one of the most unusual novels I've read in years." *Bay Area Reporter*, San Francisco.

"Exotic locations, high-powered wheeling and dealing and excursions into this new world's dark underside . . . make this a book that captures the imagination and will not let it go until the last page." *Out in Jersey* Magazine.
312 pages, $16.95, 2008,
ISBN 978-1-892149-05-3

At Your Bookstore, or from:

Belhue Press
2501 Palisade Avenue, Suite A1
Bronx, NY 10463

E-mail: belhuepress@earthlink.net
Please add $3.50 shipping for the first book and $1.00 for each book thereafter. New York State residents please add 8.25% sales tax. Foreign orders in U.S. currency only.
You can now order Perry Brass's exciting books online at www.perrybrass.com.
Please visit this website for more details, regular updates, and news of future events and books.